Verbal Reasoning

The 11+
10-Minute Tests

Ages
10-11

Practise • Prepare • Pass

Everything your child needs for 11+ success

How to use this book

This book is made up of 10-minute tests and puzzle pages.
There are answers and detailed explanations in the pull-out section at the back of the book.

10-Minute Tests

- There are 37 tests in this book, each containing either 14 or 16 questions.
  Each test is a bite-sized version of a full-length 11+ test.

- Each test is designed to cover a good range of the question styles and topics that
  your child could come across in their 11+ test, at the same difficulty level.

- Your child should aim to score at least 12 out of 14 or 14 out of 16 in each 10-minute test.
  If they score less than this, use their results to work out the areas they need more practice on.

- If your child hasn't managed to finish the test in time, they need to work on increasing their
  speed, whereas if they have made a lot of mistakes, they need to work more carefully.

- Keep track of your child's scores using the progress chart on the inside back cover of the book.

Puzzle Pages

- There are 10 puzzle pages in this book, which are a great break from test-style questions.
  They encourage children to practise the same skills that they will need in the test,
  but in a fun way.

Published by CGP

Editors:
Rachel Grocott, Heather McClelland, Sabrina Robinson

With thanks to Holly Poynton and Judy Hornigold for the proofreading.

ISBN: 978 1 78294 258 0
Printed by Elanders Ltd, Newcastle upon Tyne
Clipart from Corel®

Based on the classic CGP style created by Richard Parsons.

Contents

You have **10 minutes** to do this test. Work as quickly and accurately as you can.

Find the letter that will finish the first word and start the second word of each pair. The same letter must be used for both pairs.

Example: par (?) een   bac (?) ept   (___k___)

---

1. hur (?) ean   boi (?) awn   (_____)

2. rai (?) ial   pro (?) ark   (_____)

3. war (?) ore   cal (?) ost   (_____)

4. car (?) ars   isl (?) arl   (_____)

Choose the word that has a similar meaning to the words in both sets of brackets. Underline your answer.

Example: (twig   branch)   (fasten   attach)   glue   <u>stick</u>   trunk   affix   bough

---

5. (role   character)   (separate   divide)   play   split   cast   part

6. (hut   outhouse)   (remove   discard)   shed   strip   moult   annex

7. (adjourn   postpone) (hang   dangle)   delay   suspend   drape   droop

8. (reserve   order)   (novel   hardback)   purchase   story   buy   book

Find the missing number to complete each sum. Write your answer on the line.

Example: $7 + 5 = 24 \div ($ ___2___ $)$

9. $15 + 4 = 29 - ($ _____ $)$

10. $30 \div 5 + 12 = 2 \times ($ _____ $)$

11. $7 + 4 - 8 = 33 \div ($ _____ $)$

12. $12 \div 4 \times 6 = 2 \times ($ _____ $)$

Underline the pair of letters that completes each sentence in the most sensible way. Use the alphabet to help you.

A B C D E F G H I J K L M N O P Q R S T U V W X Y Z

Example: DG is to **FE** as **RU** is to (<u>TS</u> SR TU ST US).

13. **GJ** is to **OL** as **OQ** is to (WU XU XS VY WS).

14. **HF** is to **DJ** as **NL** is to (JP IO KQ JO PK).

15. **FR** is to **MN** as **RM** is to (XI YJ YI XH ZJ).

16. **BI** is to **HC** as **JQ** is to (OK QK PL PJ PK).

END OF TEST

/ 16

3

You have **10 minutes** to do this test. Work as quickly and accurately as you can.

Remove one letter from the first word and add it to the second word to make two new words. Do not change the order of the other letters. Write the letter that moves on the line.

Example: claw   age   (___C___)   (The new words are **law** and **cage**.)

---

1. glade   pin   (_____)

2. heart   tip   (_____)

3. clean   row   (_____)

4. found   ant   (_____)

Underline two words, one from each set of brackets, that have the most opposite meaning.

Example: (eager <u>happy</u> curious)   (tired <u>sad</u> unwell)

---

5. (acknowledge venerate celebrate)   (deject commiserate dissatisfy)

6. (victimise chastise contest)   (commend probe vindicate)

7. (minute untraceable inconsequential) (protruding definable paramount)

8. (demonic hostile heinous)   (refined angelic tenacious)

4

Find the missing number to complete each sum. Write your answer on the line.

Example: $7 + 5 = 24 \div (\underline{\quad 2 \quad})$

9. $8 \times 4 = 64 \div (\underline{\qquad})$

10. $100 \div 5 = 3 \times (\underline{\qquad}) + 2$

11. $21 \div 7 + 3 = 66 \div (\underline{\qquad})$

12. $40 - 30 + 20 = 3 \times (\underline{\qquad})$

Each question uses a different code. Use the alphabet to help you work out the answer to each question.

A B C D E F G H I J K L M N O P Q R S T U V W X Y Z

Example: If the code for **MANY** is **LZMX**, what is the code for **GREY**? ($\underline{\text{FQDX}}$)

13. If the code for **BONE** is **DMPC**, what is the code for **MARK**? ($\underline{\qquad}$)

14. If the code for **CALM** is **ZEIQ**, what is the code for **VOTE**? ($\underline{\qquad}$)

15. If the code for **DICE** is **BGAC**, what is **PYEC** the code for? ($\underline{\qquad}$)

16. If the code for **FLAN** is **EJXJ**, what is **FPFZ** the code for? ($\underline{\qquad}$)

END OF TEST

/ 16

Time for a break! These puzzles are a great way to practise your **coding** skills.

Crack the Code to find the Treasure

In the table below, each letter of the alphabet is represented by the numbers 1-26. Complete the table to reveal the code.

A	B	C	D	E	F	G	H	I	J	K	L	M	N	O	P	Q	R	S	T	U	V	W	X	Y	Z
			11						5				1	26						20					

Now use the code to complete the instructions below. Follow the instructions to find the hidden treasure!

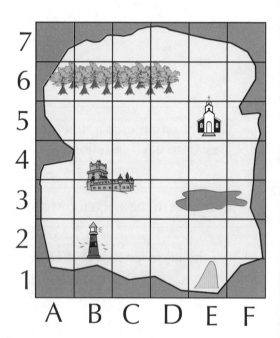

a) Start at the (**7, 6, 3, 3**).

b) Go up (**9, 6, 19, 10**) squares.

c) Go (**11, 26, 18, 1**) one square.

d) Go (**3, 10, 9, 21**) three squares.

e) Go down (**21, 7, 23, 10, 10**) squares to find the treasure.

The treasure is buried under the

_____.

Find the Hidden Word

In the sentence below, a six-letter word is hidden at the end of one word and the start of the next. Underline the part of the sentence that contains the hidden word and write the hidden word on the dotted line.

Pirate Pete is deliberating between basil versus sage for his pasta sauce.

Hidden word: _ _ _ _ _ _

Test 3

You have **10 minutes** to do this test. Work as quickly and accurately as you can.

In each sentence below, a four-letter word is hidden at the end of one word and the start of the next. Write the hidden word on the line.

Example: We were flying <u>low</u> below the clouds.   (<u>glow</u>)

---

1. She often likes to cycle anticlockwise.   (_____)

2. What does the mouse usually eat?   (_____)

3. The seal hopes to catch some mackerel.   (_____)

4. Bring those atlases over here now!   (_____)

Choose the word that has a similar meaning to the words in both sets of brackets. Underline your answer.

Example: (twig   branch)   (fasten   attach)   glue   <u>stick</u>   trunk   affix   bough

---

5. (flee   run)   (fasten   secure)   dash   lock   bolt   jog   rivet

6. (babysit   supervise) (intellect   brain)   tend   imagination   mind   sense

7. (sour   acidic)   (resentful   hateful)   bitter   mean   severe   disagreeable

8. (type   sort)   (friendly   considerate)   class   variety   obliging   kind

9. Rosie, Rachael, Susannah, Amélie and James had a competition to see who could bake the widest cookies. Rosie's cookies were over 1.1 m wide. Rachael's cookies were only half as wide. Susannah and Amélie both baked their cookies for 30 minutes. James's cookies were the widest by 23 cm.

    If the statements above are true, only one of the sentences below **must** be true. Which one? Circle the correct letter.

    A   Rachael's cookies were the smallest.
    B   Susannah and Amélie's cookies were the same width.
    C   Rosie's cookies were the widest.
    D   Rachael's cookies were not the second widest.
    E   Rosie's cookies were the second widest.

10. A department store has five departments across three floors. The departments include toys, gifts, children's wear, men's wear and women's wear. The first floor has two departments. Gifts are on the top floor. The toy department is located next to children's wear. Men's wear is not on the ground floor, which only has one department.

    If the statements above are true, only one of the sentences below **cannot** be true. Which one? Circle the correct letter.

    A   The gift department is directly above women's wear.
    B   Men's wear is next to the gifts.
    C   Women's wear is on the ground floor.
    D   The first floor has two departments.
    E   The ground floor is the only floor with one department.

Find the missing number to complete each sum. Write your answer on the line.

Example: $7 + 5 = 24 \div (\underline{\quad 2 \quad})$

11. $7 \times 2 = 10 + (\underline{\qquad})$

12. $18 \div 3 = 4 \times (\underline{\qquad}) - 2$

13. $9 \times 3 + 8 = 7 \times (\underline{\qquad})$

14. $5 + 5 + 7 = 60 \div (\underline{\qquad}) - 3$

END OF TEST

/ 14

You have **10 minutes** to do this test. Work as quickly and accurately as you can.

Find the three-letter word that completes the word in capital letters, and so finishes the sentence in a sensible way. Write your answer on the line.

Example: It can be **CHY** outside when it snows.   (<u>ILL</u>)

---

1. He **SWALED** the custard quickly.   (_____)

2. I **SLD** my finger open cutting the bread.   (_____)

3. He wasn't happy and asked for a **RED**.   (_____)

4. The burglar **TARED** the expensive mansion.   (_____)

Three of the words in each list are linked. Underline the two words that are **not** related to these three.

Example: puppy   kitten   <u>duck</u>   calf   <u>sheep</u>

---

5. famine   lack   drought   scarcity   shortage

6. victorious   triumphant   fulfilment   accomplishment   success

7. happy   sympathetic   content   delighted   understanding

8. envelope   card   stamp   letter   address

9. beautiful   stunning   atmospheric   striking   ethereal

10

Find the number that completes the final set of numbers in the same way as the first two sets. Write your answer on the line.

Example: 7 (4) 3   10 (5) 5   15 (__11__) 4

10. 7 (10) 3   12 (14) 2   17 (_____) 7

11. 3 (9) 6   4 (16) 8   6 (_____) 5

12. 4 (10) 2   5 (17) 3   4 (_____) 6

13. 4 (12) 2   5 (16) 3   6 (_____) 4

The number codes for three of these four words are listed in a random order. Work out the code to answer the questions.

TEAL   LATE   EAST   STAY
3564   1543   6452

14. Find the code for the word **LATE**.   (_____)

15. Find the code for the word **SEAT**.   (_____)

16. Find the word that has the number code **4513**. (_____)

END OF TEST

/ 16

You have **10 minutes** to do this test. Work as quickly and accurately as you can.

> The words in the second set follow the same pattern as the words in the first set. Find the missing word to complete the second set. Write the answer on the line.
>
> **Example:** gate (tie) lid   boat (**art**) arm

1. frog (rode) dent   stir (_time_) mean

2. rate (rail) ill   song (_some_) met

3. date (tale) vile   milk (_list_) waft

4. wade (awe) crew   trio (_ram_) coma

> Choose two words, one from each set of brackets, that complete the sentence in the most sensible way. Underline both words.
>
> **Example:** **Library** is to (book <u>read</u> quietly) as **bakery** is to (baker tasty <u>bake</u>).

5. **Apples** are to (<u>tree</u> pie forest) as **blackberries** are to (fruit <u>bush</u> pick).

6. **Blizzard** is to (<u>snow</u> freezing cold) as **hurricane** is to (blustery <u>wind</u> tornado).

7. **Nibble** is to (munch teeth <u>eat</u>) as **sip** is to (<u>drink</u> liquid straw).

8. **Pilot** is to (<u>airport</u> aviation runway) as **choreographer** is to (<u>dance</u> ballet dancer).

Each letter stands for a number. Work out the answer to each sum as a letter. Write your answer on the line.

Example: A = 1 B = 2 C = 6 D = 12 E = 10 $D \div B = ($ ___C___ $)$

9. A = 3 B = 5 C = 6 D = 14 E = 19 $A + B + C = ($ _D_ $)$

10. A = 2 B = 3 C = 8 D = 10 E = 15 $E \div B + D = ($ _E_ $)$

11. A = 1 B = 4 C = 8 D = 32 E = 64 $D \div C \times A = ($ _B_ $)$

12. A = 2 B = 4 C = 12 D = 20 E = 24 $E \div C \times A + D = ($ _E_ $)$

Underline the pair of letters that completes each sentence in the most sensible way. Use the alphabet to help you.

A B C D E F G H I J K L M N O P Q R S T U V W X Y Z

Example: **DG** is to **FE** as **RU** is to (<u>TS</u> SR TU ST US).

13. **BY** is to **DW** as **FU** is to (CX HS GT HT EV).

14. **EF** is to **IN** as **GH** is to (KP KR KL JK LK).

15. **CG** is to **XT** as **EI** is to (WR VS VR UQ US).

16. **CG** is to **HE** as **TX** is to (ZW YV YU ZV XV).

END OF TEST

13 / 16

13

You have **10 minutes** to do this test. Work as quickly and accurately as you can.

> Underline a word from the first set, followed by a word from the second set, that go together to form a new word.
>
> **Example:** (<u>water</u> suggest disc)   (<u>fall</u> hard ton)   (The word is **waterfall**.)

1. (with all where)   (though out ever)

2. (hell handle by)   (met cycle bar)

3. (cot miss comb)   (shun tun at)

4. (disc per inn)   (chase cushion form)

> Underline two words, one from each set of brackets, that have the most similar meaning.
>
> **Example:** (cream treat <u>dessert</u>)   (cake <u>pudding</u> delicious)

5. (jog amble skip)   (stroll sprint race)

6. (fall drop disintegrate)   (explode down crumble)

7. (relish eat mouth)   (digest savour food)

8. (tranquil quiet rest)   (relax noise soothe)

14

Find the pair of letters that continues each sequence in the best way. Use the alphabet to help you.

A B C D E F G H I J K L M N O P Q R S T U V W X Y Z

Example: TU   QR   NO   KL   HI   (__EF__)

9. BB   CC   EE   HH   LL   (_____)

10. LC   KD   IF   FI   BM   (_____)

11. VD   UG   UJ   VM   XP   (_____)

12. CA   EB   GC   IE   KH   (_____)

Each question uses a different code. Use the alphabet to help you work out the answer to each question.

A B C D E F G H I J K L M N O P Q R S T U V W X Y Z

Example: If the code for **MANY** is **LZMX**, what is the code for **GREY**? (__FQDX__)

13. If the code for **BATH** is **EDWK**, what is the code for **HELP**?   (_____)

14. If the code for **BEAR** is **XAWN**, what is **YHEL** the code for?   (_____)

15. If the code for **DEAF** is **WVZU**, what is the code for **FROG**?   (_____)

16. If the code for **FROWN** is **GTRAS**, what is **QQDGM** the code for?   (_____)

END OF TEST

/ 16

15

Puzzles 2

Time for a break! These puzzles are a great way to practise your **vocabulary** skills.

Antonym Antics

Complete the crossword by choosing an appropriate **antonym** for each word below.

ACROSS

1. accept
2. different
3. quiet
4. fragile
5. earlier
6. arrogant

DOWN

1. loyal
2. imprison
3. midnight
4. clumsy
5. doubt
6. common

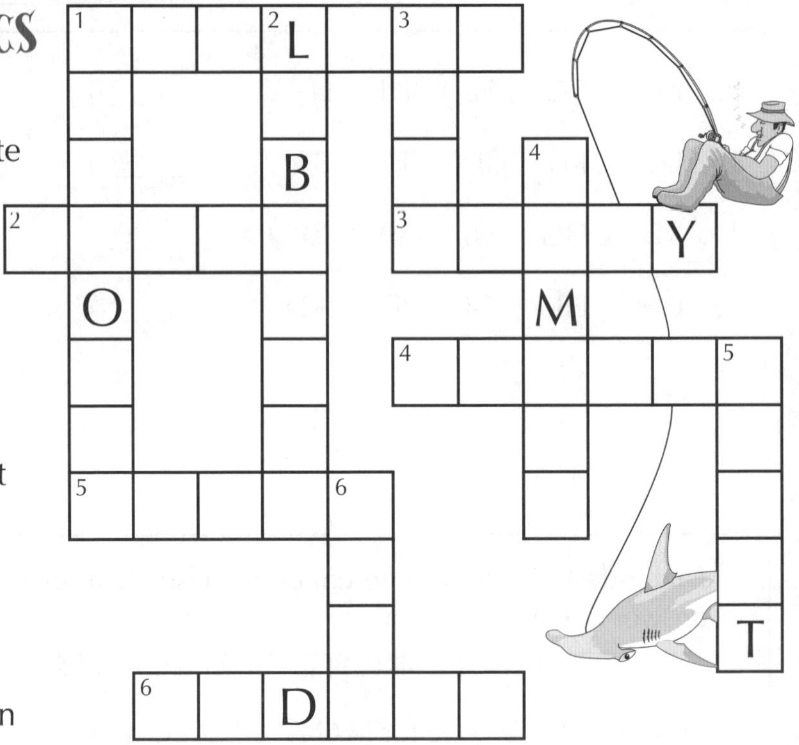

Spell and Unscramble

Each word below is misspelt. First, cross out the wrong letters, then rearrange the wrong letters into an antonym for the word **lack**.

Watch out — there may be more than one wrong letter per word.

o b b j e c t   u n n h a b i t

i n n d e p e n d a n t   s h a r c k

a p o l o d g y   t e m p a r e t u r e

Antonym of **lack**: ____________________

You have **10 minutes** to do this test. Work as quickly and accurately as you can.

Find the word that completes the third pair of words so that it follows the same pattern as the first two pairs. Write your answer on the line.

Example: boat oat   chip hip   land (_**and**_)

1. peach chap   blast stab   teach (_____)

2. centre rent   gently lent   learnt (_____)

3. knitted kite   trailed tale   snarled (_____)

4. divide dive   retake rate   chrome (_____)

Choose two words, one from each set of brackets, that complete the sentence in the most sensible way. Underline both words.

Example: Library is to (book <u>read</u> quietly) as **bakery** is to (baker tasty <u>bake</u>).

5. **Redundant** is to (retired superfluous alone) as **wilful** is to (mean rude headstrong).

6. **Demand** is to (supply stock shipment) as **question** is to (exam learn answer).

7. **Waste** is to (dispose litter smell) as **food** is to (digest hunger nutrient).

8. **Bounty** is to (generous cowboy reward) as **mirage** is to (reflect illusion mould).

9. Aadi, Becki, Catherine, Di and Ed want to see who can dive the deepest in a three-metre-deep pool. Becki missed the bottom of the pool by 140 cm. Aadi reached the bottom of the pool. Catherine dived half as deep as Aadi. Di and Ed both dived to the same depth. Neither Di nor Ed had the shallowest dive.

If the statements above are true, only one of the sentences below **must** be true. Which one? Circle the correct letter.

A Di and Ed both had the shallowest dive.

B Becki had the shallowest dive.

C Catherine dived deeper than Becki.

D Aadi had the second deepest dive.

E Catherine had the shallowest dive.

10. Carl is drawing a treasure map which is five squares wide along the bottom (A-E) and five squares high up the side (1-5). The forest is three squares north-east of the dungeon. The tower is two squares south of the castle. The dungeon is one square west of the tower. The castle is in square C4. The sand dunes are one square away from the castle and three squares away from the dungeon.

If the statements above are true, only one of the sentences below **must** be true. Which one? Circle the correct letter.

A The dungeon is not next to the village.

B The sand dunes are three squares west of the forest.

C The castle is north of the forest.

D The tower is four squares south of the sand dunes.

E The tower is intended to defend the castle.

Find the number that completes the final set of numbers in the same way as the first two sets. Write your answer on the line.

Example: 7 (4) 3   10 (5) 5   15 (__11__) 4

11. 18 (6) 3   42 (7) 6   26 (_____) 13

12. 8 (12) 6   15 (19) 6   12 (_____) 23

13. 16 (20) 6   15 (12) 9   18 (_____) 5

14. 45 (13) 5   22 (6) 11   54 (_____) 9

END OF TEST

/ 14

You have **10 minutes** to do this test. Work as quickly and accurately as you can.

> The words in the second set follow the same pattern as the words in the first set.
> Find the missing word to complete the second set. Write the answer on the line.
>
> **Example:** gate (tie) lid   boat (__*art*__) arm

1. cows (now) wind   seam (_____) pity

2. mean (ear) earl   care (_____) gate

3. opal (oar) pore   deal (_____) lame

4. dark (ran) rain   film (_____) trod

> The number codes for three of these four words are listed in a random order.
> Work out the code to answer the questions.

PORT   TEAR   TORE   ROPE

6213   4356   1264

5. Find the code for the word **PORT**.   (_____)

6. Find the code for the word **TRAP**.   (_____)

7. Find the word that has the number code **6543**. (_____)

Choose the word that has a similar meaning to the words in both sets of brackets. Underline your answer.

Example: (twig   branch)   (fasten   attach)   glue   <u>stick</u>   trunk   affix   bough

8. (expensive costly) (cherished beloved) treasured dear valued overpriced

9. (business trade)   (habit tradition)   custom routine shop norm office

10. (quick speedy)   (secured stable)   mobile fixed attached rash fast

11. (display monitor) (test examine)   auditor image proof screen trial

Each letter stands for a number. Work out the answer to each sum as a letter. Write your answer on the line.

Example: A = 1   B = 2   C = 6   D = 12   E = 10   D ÷ B = (__C__)

12. A = 3   B = 5   C = 15   D = 20   E = 25   B × A + B = (_____)

13. A = 1   B = 3   C = 7   D = 8   E = 17   B × D − C = (_____)

14. A = 2   B = 5   C = 8   D = 10   E = 12   C + A − B = (_____)

15. A = 3   B = 5   C = 7   D = 11   E = 15   E ÷ A + B − C = (_____)

16. A = 2   B = 4   C = 6   D = 8   E = 9   C × A ÷ B + C = (_____)

END OF TEST

/ 16

You have **10 minutes** to do this test. Work as quickly and accurately as you can.

Remove one letter from the first word and add it to the second word to make two new words. Do not change the order of the other letters. Write the letter that moves on the line.

Example: claw   age   (___C___)   (The new words are **law** and **cage**.)

---

1. chain   rod   (_____)

2. least   bid   (_____)

3. mince   lot   (_____)

4. plane   wok   (_____)

Underline two words, one from each set of brackets, that have the most opposite meaning.

Example: (eager <u>happy</u> curious)   (tired <u>sad</u> unwell)

---

5. (energize tantalize inspire)   (desensitize tire frustrate)

6. (erode smudge dishevel)   (groom remodel sluice)

7. (dampen extinguish neutralize)   (spark ignite fuel)

8. (engrossed aloof altruistic)   (earnest egocentric unique)

Find the word that completes the third pair of words so that it follows the same pattern as the first two pairs. Write your answer on the line.

Example: boat oat   chip hip   land (_**and**_)

9. halves save   dancer race   baking   (_____)

10. battle late   forest sort   celery   (_____)

11. raider raid   distil list   jailer   (_____)

12. craft draft   seam team   blue   (_____)

Find the number that continues each sequence in the best way. Write your answer on the line.

Example: 3   6   9   12   15   (_**18**_)

13. 34   28   22   16   10   (_____)

14. 81   27   9   3   (_____)

15. 8   9   11   14   18   (_____)

16. 6   20   10   16   14   12   (_____)

END OF TEST

/ 16

You have **10 minutes** to do this test. Work as quickly and accurately as you can.

> Underline a word from the first set, followed by a word from the second set, that go together to form a new word.
>
> **Example:** (<u>water</u> suggest disc) (<u>fall</u> hard ton) (The word is **waterfall**.)

1. (add consent horse) (rated here radish)

2. (so fore waste) (bid lid full)

3. (wretch trait lime) (light tour shed)

4. (wretch trait no) (vice tour shed)

5. (tie consider whole) (some rant ration)

> Choose the word that has a similar meaning to the words in both sets of brackets. Underline your answer.
>
> **Example:** (twig branch) (fasten attach) glue <u>stick</u> trunk affix bough

6. (slant incline) (slender thin) skinny slope lean tilt slim

7. (instance occurrence) (container box) case cover example jacket sleeve

8. (eminent famous) (recorded written) known minuted noted great grand

9. (undiluted pure) (tidy orderly) dapper unmixed true distilled neat

Find the number that completes the final set of numbers in the same way as the first two sets. Write your answer on the line.

Example: 7 (4) 3   10 (5) 5   15 (__11__) 4

10. 7 (13) 4   3 (21) 16   15 (_____) 8

11. 4 (28) 7   13 (26) 2   8 (_____) 12

12. 20 (3) 5   48 (5) 8   22 (_____) 11

13. 20 (9) 5   8 (6) 2   12 (_____) 6

The number codes for three of these four words are listed in a random order. Work out the code to answer the questions.

GRID   GEAR   DRAG   ARID
1364   5461   6425

14. Find the code for the word **GRID**.   (_____)

15. Find the code for the word **DARE**.   (_____)

16. Find the word that has the number code **5243**. (_____)

END OF TEST

/ 16

There are two puzzles on this page that are bound to give your brain a work out.

Find the Secret Message

Find the two words that should be swapped in order for each sentence to make sense. Underline both words and write them in the box below.

Rearrange the words you've underlined to reveal a secret message.

1. The robbers broke in at gold and stole the queen's midnight.
2. Hopefully the order delivered be will on Tuesday morning.
3. At clown the Jane's party was very funny.
4. Mum's pork be will eventually medallions ready to eat.

Secret message: _____

_____.

Wordy Wisdom

Solve the clues to find out something about Harry the hippo.

a. Find a multiple of four whose letters are in alphabetical order.
b. Replace the first letter of your answer with the letter that's nine places after 'J' in the alphabet.
c. Add a letter that sounds like a vegetable between the first two letters.

   Answer: Harry isn't very _____.

26

⏱ 10

You have **10 minutes** to do this test. Work as quickly and accurately as you can.

Find the letter that will finish the first word and start the second word of each pair. The same letter must be used for both pairs.

Example: par (?) een   bac (?) ept   (__k__)

---

1. clas (?) lug   sto (?) eer   (_____)

2. boo (?) ind   ban (?) ing   (_____)

3. her (?) ark   com (?) ear   (_____)

4. fee (?) ime   cur (?) ard   (_____)

Underline two words, one from each set of brackets, that have the most similar meaning.

Example: (cream treat <u>dessert</u>)   (cake <u>pudding</u> delicious)

---

5. (wealth hoard prosper)   (stockpile amass surplus)

6. (ramble cross debate)   (mumble babble abridge)

7. (scour saunter cruise)   (traverse cross wander)

8. (discard dispose eject)   (expel erupt radiate)

27

9. Five keys are broken on the Smiths' keyboard. Dad can type TRADE, but he can't type GRAND. Mum can type CLEAR, but she can't type THICK. Granny can type TACKS, but she can't type LOUSE. Granddad can type CLAPS, but he can't type HIRES. Aunty can type GUARD, but she can't type CITED.

    If the statements above are true, only one of the sentences below **cannot** be true. Which one? Circle the correct letter.

    A   From the information given, it isn't possible to name all 5 broken keys.

    B   The letters 'N' and 'I' are broken.

    C   It is possible to write the word GRAPH.

    D   The letter 'H' definitely doesn't work.

    E   It isn't possible to write the word CLOCK.

10. Ailsa, Corinne, Elgar, Gajra and Isobel are measuring worms during a science lesson. Ailsa's worm is 21 cm long. Corinne's worm is double this length. Elgar's worm is the length of Ailsa and Isobel's worms added together. Isobel's worm is one-third of the length of Ailsa's. Isobel's worm is not the shortest.

    If the statements above are true, only one of the sentences below **must** be true. Which one? Circle the correct letter.

    A   Isobel's worm is the second longest.

    B   Gajra's worm is the shortest.

    C   Elgar's worm is the third longest.

    D   Corinne's worm is the second longest.

    E   Ailsa's worm is the shortest.

Underline a word from the first set, followed by a word from the second set, that go together to form a new word.

Example: (<u>water</u> suggest disc)   (<u>fall</u> hard ton)   (The word is **waterfall**.)

11. (what   some   time)   (where   why   here)

12. (break   pop   corks)   (screw   king   corn)

13. (sty   fore   back)   (clog   led   cake)

14. (tie   gaze   rein)   (force   storm   bow)

END OF TEST

/ 14

You have **10 minutes** to do this test. Work as quickly and accurately as you can.

Find the pair of letters that continues each sequence in the best way. Use the alphabet to help you.

A B C D E F G H I J K L M N O P Q R S T U V W X Y Z

Example: TU   QR   NO   KL   HI   (__EF__)

---

1. FI   HK   HJ   JL   JK   (_____)

2. CR   DQ   FO   IL   MH   (_____)

3. AI   CK   GM   MO   UQ   (_____)

4. BC   EB   HA   KZ   NY   (_____)

Underline the pair of letters that completes each sentence in the most sensible way. Use the alphabet to help you.

A B C D E F G H I J K L M N O P Q R S T U V W X Y Z

Example: **DG** is to **FE** as **RU** is to (<u>TS</u>   SR   TU   ST   US).

---

5. **CH** is to **FK** as **LQ** is to (NS   OT   OS   OU   PT)

6. **DW** is to **ET** as **GU** is to (IR   IU   HR   HS   IS)

7. **LN** is to **QT** as **NP** is to (RU   RV   SV   SW   SU)

8. **BF** is to **YU** as **DH** is to (VS   WR   XR   WS   XS)

Find the three-letter word that completes the word in capital letters, and so finishes the sentence in a sensible way. Write your answer on the line.

Example: It can be **CHY** outside when it snows.   (_ILL_)

9.   I scored ten points when I got the ball in the **BET**.   (_____)

10. The cheese has to be **CONED** by Tuesday.   (_____)

11. She unfairly took all the **CIT**.   (_____)

12. You'll need to **ADE** to the plan.   (_____)

Three of the words in each list are linked. Underline the two words that are **not** related to these three.

Example: puppy   kitten   <u>duck</u>   calf   <u>sheep</u>

13. biscuit   milk   juice   apple   water

14. write   doodle   draw   compose   sketch

15. fry   grate   boil   chop   simmer

16. dive   fly   paddle   soar   flap

END OF TEST

/ 16

Test 12

You have **10 minutes** to do this test. Work as quickly and accurately as you can.

Find the letter that will finish the first word and start the second word of each pair. The same letter must be used for both pairs.

Example: par (?) een   bac (?) ept   (___k___)

1. bu (?) ore   we (?) ry   (_____)

2. car (?) rim   cu (?) ame   (_____)

3. loa (?) ear   bu (?) ail   (_____)

4. pi (?) en   pu (?) ain   (_____)

Find the pair of letters that continues each sequence in the best way. Use the alphabet to help you.

A B C D E F G H I J K L M N O P Q R S T U V W X Y Z

Example: TU   QR   NO   KL   HI   (__EF__)

5. HN   IS   KX   NC   RH   (_____)

6. AB   DY   GA   JX   MZ   (_____)

7. DH   CL   AP   ZT   XX   (_____)

8. EG   DJ   AL   ZO   WQ   (_____)

32

Find the word that completes the third pair of words so that it follows the same pattern as the first two pairs. Write your answer on the line.

Example: boat oat   chip hip   land (_and_)

9.   tool lot   term met   gild (_____)

10. came dame   lime mime   sang (_____)

11. feeble beef   plater trap   proper (_____)

12. hearer hear   muscat mast   byroad (_____)

Choose two words, one from each set of brackets, that complete the sentence in the most sensible way. Underline both words.

Example: Library is to (book <u>read</u> quietly) as **bakery** is to (baker tasty <u>bake</u>).

13. **Complete** is to (finish lastly finally) as **start** is to (first initial begin).

14. **Brave** is to (daring courage fearlessly) as **scared** is to (fear creepy frighten).

15. **Window** is to (glass transparent clear) as **blackboard** is to (opaque wall dark).

16. **Stop** is to (slowly pause brake) as **go** is to (accelerate speed velocity).

END OF TEST

/ 16

You have **10 minutes** to do this test. Work as quickly and accurately as you can.

Find the number that continues each sequence in the best way. Write your answer on the line.

Example: 3   6   9   12   15   (__18__)

1.   4   5   7   10   14   19   (_____)

2.   9   16   25   36   49   (_____)

3.   2   6   15   31   56   (_____)

4.   31   30   30   32   29   34   (_____)

The number codes for three of these four words are listed in a random order. Work out the code to answer the questions.

RODE   READ   DARE   ROTA
4312   1653   1642

5.   Find the code for the word **READ**.   (_____)

6.   Find the code for the word **DOOR**.   (_____)

7.   Find the word that has the number code **1352**. (_____)

In each sentence below, a four-letter word is hidden at the end of one word and the start of the next. Write the hidden word on the line.

Example: We were flying <u>low</u> below the clouds. (<u>glow</u>)

8.   Let's wait for him by the arch.   (_____)

9.   I shall shear my sheep tomorrow.   (_____)

10. How many owls are living in the barn? (_____)

11. She had artefacts all around the house. (_____)

Underline two words, one from each set of brackets, that have the most opposite meaning.

Example: (eager <u>happy</u> curious)   (tired <u>sad</u> unwell)

12. (oppose   debate   disallow)   (enjoy   accept   reward)

13. (problematic   deconstruct   break)   (resolve   repair   solution)

14. (ornate   beautiful   woven)   (plain   neglected   menacing)

15. (enormous   large   sizeable)   (average   undersized   minuscule)

16. (sleeping   sit   idle)   (runner   active   upright)

END OF TEST

/ 16

35   Test 14

Have a break! These puzzles are a great way to practise your **word** and **coding** skills.

Synonym Snake

Fill in the Synonym Snake with a synonym for each word below. Each synonym starts with the last letter of the previous synonym. The first and last letters of each word are given in the grey boxes.

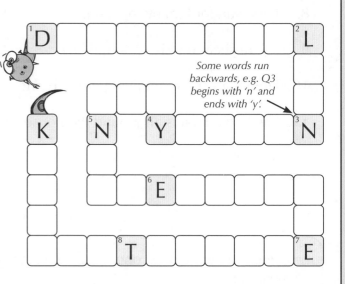

Some words run backwards, e.g. Q3 begins with 'n' and ends with 'y'.

1. lovely
2. slim
3. inform
4. crave

5. innocent
6. guess
7. obvious
8. cooperation

Crack the Code

Rachel is a member of a secret club. Once a week they meet in Rachel's shed to discuss secret matters. To get into the shed, each member has to say the right password, and the password changes every week. To find out what the new password is, members have to use the secret code.

Look at last week's code and the password to work out what this week's password will be. If you get stuck, there's a clue at the bottom of the page.

Last week's code: 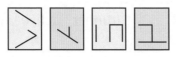   Last week's password: <u>WASP</u>

This week's code:

This week's password: ___ ___ ___ ___ ___ ___ ___

Clue: Turn the page 90 degrees clockwise.

You have **10 minutes** to do this test. Work as quickly and accurately as you can.

Remove one letter from the first word and add it to the second word to make two new words. Do not change the order of the other letters. Write the letter that moves on the line.

Example: claw   age   (___C___)   (The new words are **law** and **cage**.)

1. chink   now   (_____)

2. wince   hip   (_____)

3. booth   hop   (_____)

4. weave   pot   (_____)

Choose the word that has a similar meaning to the words in both sets of brackets. Underline your answer.

Example: (twig   branch)   (fasten   attach)   glue   <u>stick</u>   trunk   affix   bough

5. (port   dock)   (shelter   hide)   protect marine conceal quay harbour

6. (hit   spar)   (carton   container)   thump package fight box slap

7. (rubbish   waste)   (decline   reject)   spurn refuse litter debris disdain

8. (assign   entrust)   (emissary   envoy)   delegate consign bequeath give help

Find the number that completes the final set of numbers in the same way as the first two sets. Write your answer on the line.

Example: 7 (4) 3   10 (5) 5   15 (__11__) 4

9. 4 (16) 4   3 (27) 9   7 (_____) 11

10. 15 (20) 25   9 (12) 15   14 (_____) 18

11. 12 (17) 7   10 (14) 6   16 (_____) 6

12. 2 (3) 6   6 (9) 6   14 (_____) 2

Read the information carefully, then use it to answer the question that follows.

13. Luke, Finn, Sara, Ramon and Mireia are discussing which vegetables they like. Luke only likes broccoli and cabbage. Finn's favourite vegetable is carrots. Sara only likes carrots, cauliflower, broccoli and cabbage. Mireia likes more types of vegetable than Sara. Ramon dislikes all types of vegetable.

If the statements above are true, only one of the sentences below **must** be true. Which one? Circle the correct letter.

A   Ramon likes the most types of vegetable.

B   Luke likes more types of vegetable than Mireia.

C   Luke likes more types of vegetable than Finn.

D   Finn likes more types of vegetable than Ramon.

E   Sara likes more types of vegetable than Finn.

14. Two groups of children are baking cakes following a recipe that uses eggs, flour, butter, sugar and baking powder. Neil, Hugo and Aaron are in Group 1, and Pria, Wayne and Nancy are in Group 2. Neil has eggs and chocolate chips. Wayne has butter and sugar. Pria has sugar and baking powder. Aaron has butter and flour. Nancy has baking powder and raisins. Hugo has flour and eggs.

If the statements above are true, only one of the sentences below cannot be true. Which one? Circle the correct letter.

A   If Hugo swaps groups with Pria, both groups will be able to bake.

B   Neither group has the right combination of ingredients.

C   Group 1 is missing two ingredients.

D   If Wayne swaps his sugar for Neil's eggs, Group 2 will be able to bake.

E   Group 2 has more sugar than it needs for the cakes.

END OF TEST

/ 14

You have **10 minutes** to do this test. Work as quickly and accurately as you can.

Choose two words, one from each set of brackets, that complete the sentence in the most sensible way. Underline both words.

Example: **Library** is to (book <u>read</u> quietly) as **bakery** is to (baker tasty <u>bake</u>).

1. **Toothpaste** is to (tube brush soft) as **juice** is to (water flow carton).

2. **Scanty** is to (dress meagre cold) as **opulent** is to (luxurious royalty riches).

3. **Midwife** is to (nurse deliver hospital) as **lumberjack** is to (fell axe tree).

4. **Planet** is to (distant orbit spherical) as **cloud** is to (float rain heaven).

Underline the pair of letters that completes each sentence in the most sensible way. Use the alphabet to help you.

A B C D E F G H I J K L M N O P Q R S T U V W X Y Z

Example: **DG** is to **FE** as **RU** is to (<u>TS</u> SR TU ST US).

5. **BK** is to **EO** as **MR** is to (OV   PU   PV   QU   OW).

6. **PS** is to **ON** as **HT** is to (IQ   GO   FQ   IO   GP).

7. **WZ** is to **ZT** as **MS** is to (PN   PM   QL   OM   QN).

8. **FA** is to **UZ** as **LG** is to (TP   OP   QS   OT   PU).

Underline a word from the first set, followed by a word from the second set, that go together to form a new word.

Example: (<u>water</u> suggest disc) (<u>fall</u> hard ton) (The word is **waterfall**.)

9. (habit car prim)   (rose rage tat)

10. (dead scare hurry)   (let cane lock)

11. (skill ten self)   (don fish full)

12. (yell side try)   (board low angle)

Find the number that completes the final set of numbers in the same way as the first two sets. Write your answer on the line.

Example: 7 (4) 3   10 (5) 5   15 (__11__) 4

13. 12 (17) 5   19 (27) 8   14 (_____) 7

14. 8 (8) 4   18 (9) 6   48 (_____) 8

15. 21 (1) 7   24 (4) 4   54 (_____) 9

16. 3 (7) 1   12 (32) 8   11 (_____) 8

END OF TEST

/ 16

You have **10 minutes** to do this test. Work as quickly and accurately as you can.

Find the three-letter word that completes the word in capital letters, and so finishes the sentence in a sensible way. Write your answer on the line.

Example: It can be **CHY** outside when it snows. (__ILL__)

---

1. Gran had lost her **TBLE** and pricked herself whilst sewing. (_____)

2. My notes are in one of those blue **FERS** on the top shelf. (_____)

3. The ballerinas danced across the **SLIT** stage. (_____)

4. Ian is one of the best **AEUR** tennis players in the country. (_____)

Underline two words, one from each set of brackets, that have the most opposite meaning.

Example: (eager <u>happy</u> curious)   (tired <u>sad</u> unwell)

---

5. (rescue unleash relinquish)   (restrain caution sentence)

6. (draconian bullish vain)   (reverent harmonious merciful)

7. (befuddled onerous forlorn)   (jovial determined ostentatious)

8. (acclaim heed provision)   (detestation infamy flaw)

The words in the second set follow the same pattern as the words in the first set. Find the missing word to complete the second set. Write the answer on the line.

Example: gate (tie) lid   boat (__art__) arm

9.   team (pet) hope   tear   (_____) cold

10. fawn (tan) note   bard (_____) loft

11. bail (lie) rile   feed (_____) grew

12. reef (elf) felt   pile   (_____) lark

Find the pair of letters that continues each sequence in the best way. Use the alphabet to help you.

A B C D E F G H I J K L M N O P Q R S T U V W X Y Z

Example: TU   QR   NO   KL   HI   (__EF__)

13. OP   RR   UT   XV   AX   (_____)

14. KL   MH   OD   QZ   SV   (_____)

15. PR   SQ   VO   YL   BH   (_____)

16. FH   GF   IE   LC   PB   (_____)

END OF TEST

/ 16

43

Test 18

You have **10 minutes** to do this test. Work as quickly and accurately as you can.

> Underline two words, one from each set of brackets, that have the most similar meaning.
>
> **Example:** (cream treat <u>dessert</u>) (cake <u>pudding</u> delicious)

1. (ignore hamper intervene)   (contort relay hinder)

2. (provoke force push)   (annoy tease goad)

3. (flower concertina flourish)   (thrive replicate cascade)

4. (mediocre mundane morose)   (monotonous tainted indifferent)

> The number codes for three of these four words are listed in a random order. Work out the code to answer the questions.

DARN	GEAR	AGED	DRAG
2416	6253	4125	

5. Find the code for the word **DRAG**. (_____)

6. Find the code for the word **EDGE**. (_____)

7. Find the word that has the number code **2512**. (_____)

Find the letter that will finish the first word and start the second word of each pair. The same letter must be used for both pairs.

Example: par (?) een   bac (?) ept   (___k___)

8. cas (?) eem   goa (?) our   (_____)

9. ric (?) ats   hig (?) ymn   (_____)

10. see (?) eek   pal (?) ade   (_____)

11. fla (?) ort   cla (?) aid   (_____)

12. cur (?) ear   car (?) ial   (_____)

Find the pair of letters that continues each sequence in the best way. Use the alphabet to help you.

A B C D E F G H I J K L M N O P Q R S T U V W X Y Z

Example: TU   QR   NO   KL   HI   (___EF___)

13. CF   FI   IL   LO   OR   (_____)

14. SD   WB   AZ   EX   IV   (_____)

15. VT   TU   UW   SZ   TD   (_____)

16. ZY   XB   TF   NI   FM   (_____)

END OF TEST

/ 16

Test 18

Time for a break! These puzzles are a great way to practise your **logic** skills.

Triangle Teasers

The number in each square is equal to the product of the numbers in the circles on either side.

Fill in the missing numbers.

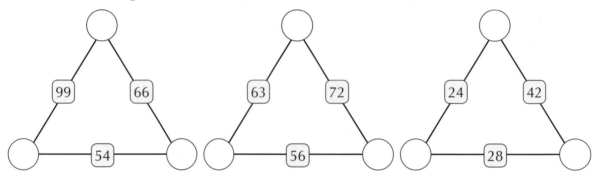

Sudoku School

Fill in the sudoku puzzle with the letters E D U C A T I O N.
Every row, column and 3x3 grid must contain the letters E D U C A T I O N, but each letter can only appear once in each row, column or 3x3 grid.

3.30 pm = home time = happy teachers ÷ no pupils

		A				U		
D	O						E	I
	I		O	A	E		T	
E			C	O	N			T
T	U	I		E		N	O	C
O			U	I	T			D
	D		A	T	U		N	
A	C						D	U
		N				O		

(10)

You have **10 minutes** to do this test. Work as quickly and accurately as you can.

Find the word that completes the third pair of words so that it follows the same pattern as the first two pairs. Write your answer on the line.

Example: boat oat   chip hip   land (__and__)

---

1. camel lame   holed dole   filet   (_____)

2. hotel hole   timer tire   coven   (_____)

3. meagre ream   hatbox oath   hacker   (_____)

4. appeal leap   rename earn   ruling   (_____)

Find the missing number to complete each sum. Write your answer on the line.

Example: $7 + 5 = 24 \div (\underline{\quad 2 \quad})$

---

5. $36 - 9 = 19 + (\underline{\qquad})$

6. $12 \times 12 = 288 \div (\underline{\qquad})$

7. $16 + 7 - 5 = 3 \times (\underline{\qquad})$

8. $47 + 3 \div 2 = 75 \div (\underline{\qquad})$

47

Three of the words in each list are linked. Underline the two words that are **not** related to these three.

Example: puppy   kitten   <u>duck</u>   calf   <u>sheep</u>

9. cough   virus   sneeze   flu   shiver

10. swimming   sailing   diving   rowing   yachting

11. eliminate   obliterate   destroy   imperil   jeopardise

12. stern   reckless   blasphemous   abrasive   harsh

Read the information carefully, then use it to answer the question that follows.

13. Sabiha, Dan, Alicia, Rodolfo and Will are running a marathon. Dan didn't finish fourth. Alicia finished before Sabiha. Will finished last. Sabiha came second.

If the statements above are true, only one of the sentences below **must** be true. Which one? Circle the correct letter.

A   Will was faster than Rodolfo.

B   Rodolfo finished fourth.

C   Alicia finished third.

D   Dan finished last.

E   Sabiha was faster than Alicia.

14. Ten Easter eggs have been hidden at five locations in a garden. These locations include a tree, a shed, a rose bush, a vegetable patch and a pond. Each location has at least one egg and no more than three eggs. There are twice as many milk chocolate eggs in the vegetable patch than there are in the shed. The vegetable patch is the only location without a dark chocolate egg. There are half as many white chocolate eggs at the tree than there are next to the pond.

If the statements above are true, only one of the sentences below **must** be true. Which one? Circle the correct letter.

A   The tree is harbouring three eggs.

B   The largest number of eggs can be found in the vegetable patch.

C   White chocolate eggs are the most popular eggs.

D   If you found all of the milk and white chocolate eggs, you'd have six eggs.

E   In total, there are six eggs hidden near the tree, the shed and the rose bush.

END OF TEST

/ 14

You have **10 minutes** to do this test. Work as quickly and accurately as you can.

> Find the three-letter word that completes the word in capital letters, and so finishes the sentence in a sensible way. Write your answer on the line.
>
> **Example:** It can be **CHY** outside when it snows. (__ILL__)

1. When the audience finished **CPING**, they called out for more. (_____)

2. Marjorie went to the dentist to have her teeth **WENED**. (_____)

3. A man in a kilt played the **BAGES** during the ceremony. (_____)

4. Dad **RECED** in horror when he saw my Halloween costume. (_____)

> Three of the words in each list are linked. Underline the two words that are **not** related to these three.
>
> **Example:** puppy kitten <u>duck</u> calf <u>sheep</u>

5. pluck roast fillet bake fry

6. consequence debrief prepay aftermath forethought

7. demote advance relegate declass upgrade

8. viewers spectators onlookers readers listeners

In each sentence below, a four-letter word is hidden at the end of one word and the start of the next. Write the hidden word on the line.

Example: We were flying <u>low</u> below the clouds. (<u>glow</u>)

9. The icicle appeared above the ledge. (_____)

10. A naughty mite managed to bite her leg. (_____)

11. The tomato salsa left a stain. (_____)

12. The civilians hid when the army attacked. (_____)

13. A great reef spans the rugged coastline. (_____)

The number codes for three of these four words are listed in a random order. Work out the code to answer the questions.

FIRE   NEAR   RAIN   FARE
3456   2645   3156

14. Find the code for the word **RAIN**. (_____)

15. Find the code for the word **RIFE**. (_____)

16. Find the word that has the number code **3126**. (_____)

END OF TEST

/ 16

⏱ 10

You have **10 minutes** to do this test. Work as quickly and accurately as you can.

Find the three-letter word that completes the word in capital letters, and so finishes the sentence in a sensible way. Write your answer on the line.

Example: It can be **CHY** outside when it snows. (<u>ILL</u>)

---

1. You need to knock down all the **STLES** to score a strike. (_____)

2. Frankie was **SLING** and gritting her teeth. (_____)

3. Tim looked **VATLY** at the teacher because he didn't understand. (_____)

4. Claire could be very cruel and often made **SEFUL** comments. (_____)

Find the number that continues each sequence in the best way. Write your answer on the line.

Example: 3   6   9   12   15 (<u>18</u>)

---

5. 54   61   68   75   82 (_____)

6. 800   400   200   100   50 (_____)

7. 11   8   15   11   19   14   23 (_____)

8. 4   12   5   10   6   8   7 (_____)

Underline two words, one from each set of brackets, that have the most opposite meaning.

Example: (eager <u>happy</u> curious)   (tired <u>sad</u> unwell)

9. (real factual belief)   (fake lie myth)

10. (secretive quiet cryptic)   (silent clear reveal)

11. (spontaneous surprise unsuspected)   (researched planned organisation)

12. (rich disgusting bland)   (wonderful delectable boring)

Each question uses a different code. Use the alphabet to help you work out the answer to each question.

A B C D E F G H I J K L M N O P Q R S T U V W X Y Z

Example: If the code for **MANY** is **LZMX**, what is the code for **GREY**? (<u>FQDX</u>)

13. If the code for **LAIR** is **OELV**, what is **FSPI** the code for? (_____)

14. If the code for **CORK** is **BOSM**, what is **RAWG** the code for? (_____)

15. If the code for **QUIT** is **UPMO**, what is the code for **FROG**? (_____)

16. If the code for **WARP** is **YEXX**, what is the code for **CLUE**? (_____)

END OF TEST

/ 16

You have **10 minutes** to do this test. Work as quickly and accurately as you can.

Find the three-letter word that completes the word in capital letters, and so finishes the sentence in a sensible way. Write your answer on the line.

Example: It can be **CHY** outside when it snows.   (__ILL__)

---

1.   Ben's mum cried when she bid him **FARLL**.   (_____)

2.   A ghost appeared at the door and **SED** everyone.   (_____)

3.   Most passwords have an **INITE** number of combinations.   (_____)

4.   The horror film was so **GSOME** that I had to change the channel.   (_____)

Each letter stands for a number. Work out the answer to each sum as a letter. Write your answer on the line.

Example: A = 1   B = 2   C = 6   D = 12   E = 10   D ÷ B = (__C__)

---

5.   A = 2   B = 4   C = 6   D = 18   E = 24   C × B = (_____)

6.   A = 4   B = 6   C = 16 D = 72   E = 80   D ÷ B + A = (_____)

7.   A = 3   B = 6   C = 7   D = 23   E = 27   C × A + B = (_____)

8.   A = 2   B = 4   C = 7   D = 9   E = 13   B × A + D − E = (_____)

Choose two words, one from each set of brackets, that complete the sentence in the most sensible way. Underline both words.

Example: **Library** is to (book <u>read</u> quietly) as **bakery** is to (baker tasty <u>bake</u>).

9. **Lecture** is to (hall students boredom) as **preach** is to (speak vicar congregation).

10. **Barter** is to (market goods bargain) as **bid** is to (gavel auction sale).

11. **Grandparent** is to (ancestor family prior) as **child** is to (youth descendent gene).

12. **Discreet** is to (secret coy unobtrusive) as **demure** is to (passive shy effeminate).

Find the missing number to complete each sum. Write your answer on the line.

Example: $7 + 5 = 24 \div (\underline{\quad 2 \quad})$

13. $39 - 16 = 14 + (\underline{\quad\quad})$

14. $9 \times 8 - 22 = 150 \div (\underline{\quad\quad})$

15. $4 + 15 - 7 = 2 \times (\underline{\quad\quad})$

16. $64 \div 8 + 8 = 4 \times (\underline{\quad\quad})$

END OF TEST

/ 16

It's puzzle time! You'll need your **word making** skills for this page.

Compound Conundrums

Nine compound words can be found in the word puzzles below. One part of
each word is given for you. Use the clues to find the second part of the words
and write the completed compound words on the lines below each puzzle.

Example:

PENCE	PENCE
PENCE	PENCE
PENCE	PENCE

<u>SIXPENCE</u>

Hint: look at what the word is <u>doing</u> or <u>how</u> it's been written. In the example,
the word 'pence' has been written six times, so the answer is 'sixpence'.

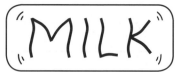

ERIF

_____   _____   _____

W I D E

_____   _____   _____

_____   _____   _____

(10)

You have **10 minutes** to do this test. Work as quickly and accurately as you can.

Find the letter that will finish the first word and start the second word of each pair. The same letter must be used for both pairs.

Example: par (?) een   bac (?) ept   (___k___)

---

1. clas (?) ale   los (?) aid   (_____)

2. bon (?) ear   all (?) our   (_____)

3. lea (?) ate   che (?) ist   (_____)

4. mai (?) ose   dow (?) ets   (_____)

Choose the word that has a similar meaning to the words in both sets of brackets. Underline your answer.

Example: (twig   branch)   (fasten   attach)   glue <u>stick</u> trunk affix bough

---

5. (shine buff)   (perfect refine)   varnish polish improve enhance

6. (limit restrict)   (cover top)   cap curtail crown curb

7. (push squeeze)   (urge compel)   impel crush drive press

8. (gesture signal)   (proposal suggestion)   sign idea motion movement

---

57

Remove one letter from the first word and add it to the second word to make two new words. Do not change the order of the other letters. Write the letter that moves on the line.

Example: claw   age   (__C__)   (The new words are **law** and **cage**.)

9. wield   sad   (_____)

10. gripe   ore   (_____)

11. witch   ape   (_____)

12. clean   hid   (_____)

Read the information carefully, then use it to answer the question that follows.

13. A gardener has planted five groups of vegetables in a circular pattern. From the circle at the centre, where the sprouts are, outwards, each group of vegetables is surrounded by another circle of vegetables of equal width. The potatoes are in the biggest ring. The cabbages are neither next to the sprouts nor the potatoes. The parsnips are closer to the cabbages than they are to the potatoes. The carrots haven't grown very well this year.

If the statements above are true, only one of the sentences below **cannot** be true. Which one? Circle the correct letter.

A   The gardener has grown more sprouts than carrots.

B   The potatoes aren't next to the parsnips.

C   The carrots are bordered by the potatoes and the cabbages.

D   Only two types of vegetable are bordered by one other type of vegetable.

E   Two rings of vegetables separate the potatoes from the sprouts.

14. Five of Jarvis's favourite programmes are on TV tomorrow on four different channels. 'Cookery Capers' starts at 9 am and lasts 90 minutes. 'Ruthless Referees' is on from 10 am to 11 am. 'Paw Pedicures' is 60 minutes long and ends at 1 pm. 'Emotional Street' starts 1 hour after 'Cookery Capers' starts, ending at the same time as 'Ruthless Referees'. 'Newscast Now' is 2 hours 30 minutes long and ends 30 minutes after 'Paw Pedicures'. Jarvis can only watch one show at a time, and he is only able to record one programme at a time.

If the statements above are true, only one of the sentences below **must** be true. Which one? Circle the correct letter.

A   'Newscast Now' lasts 60 minutes longer than 'Emotional Street'.

B   In total, Jarvis could record three complete programmes.

C   Jarvis will either miss 30 minutes of 'Emotional Street' or 30 minutes of 'Ruthless Referees' if he watches all of 'Cookery Capers'.

D   If Jarvis watches 'Ruthless Referees' and records 'Emotional Street', he would miss 60 minutes of 'Cookery Capers'.

E   Jarvis could watch the first hour of 'Newscast Now', then all of 'Paw Pedicures', followed by the remaining 15 minutes of 'Newscast Now'.

END OF TEST

/ 14

⏱ 10

You have **10 minutes** to do this test. Work as quickly and accurately as you can.

> Remove one letter from the first word and add it to the second word to make two new words. Do not change the order of the other letters. Write the letter that moves on the line.
>
> **Example:** claw   age   (___C___)   (The new words are **law** and **cage**.)

1.   acrid   dew   (_____)

2.   brand   axe   (_____)

3.   every   tub   (_____)

4.   beast   pie   (_____)

> Choose two words, one from each set of brackets, that complete the sentence in the most sensible way. Underline both words.
>
> **Example:**   **Library** is to (book <u>read</u> quietly) as **bakery** is to (baker tasty <u>bake</u>).

5.   **Cow** is to (beef calf tender) as **pig** is to (sty bacon trotter).

6.   **Season** is to (spices flavour sprinkle) as **spoon** is to (ladle liquid wooden).

7.   **Sow** is to (field seed harvest) as **indulge** is to (greed abstain luxury).

8.   **Fire** is to (mantelpiece stoke flame) as **curtain** is to (cotton night-time draw).

Find the number that continues each sequence in the best way. Write your answer on the line.

Example: 3 6 9 12 15 (__18__)

9. 35   29   24   20   17   (_____)

10. 4   6   9   14   21   32   (_____)

11. 12   20   14   16   16   12   (_____)

12. 4   8   8   4   16   2   (_____)

Underline the pair of letters that completes each sentence in the most sensible way. Use the alphabet to help you.

A B C D E F G H I J K L M N O P Q R S T U V W X Y Z

Example: **DG** is to **FE** as **RU** is to (T̲S̲ SR TU ST US).

13. **CF** is to **FG** as **TV** is to (XY   VU   WV   WW VW).

14. **KI** is to **PR** as **MQ** is to (SK   NJ   QJ   RI   SI).

15. **CK** is to **IN** as **AB** is to (GE   FF   GF   HD   FE).

16. **ZS** is to **SN** as **RM** is to (JH   LI   KH   LJ   KJ).

END OF TEST

/ 16

61

⏱ 10

You have **10 minutes** to do this test. Work as quickly and accurately as you can.

Find the word that completes the third pair of words so that it follows the same pattern as the first two pairs. Write your answer on the line.

Example: boat oat   chip hip   land (_and_)

1. barred dare   gargle earl   rowing   (_____)

2. gilded lied   popple pole   ledger   (_____)

3. complete mole   catalyse tale   comprise   (_____)

4. adhered dear   commend once   apparel   (_____)

5. rehearse hear   lethargy tear   wildness   (_____)

Underline two words, one from each set of brackets, that have the most opposite meaning.

Example: (eager happy curious)   (tired sad unwell)

6. (triumph winner goal)   (score victory field)

7. (equal agreeable unanimous)   (together joint united)

8. (match correspond connect)   (communicate cohesive identify)

9. (detached biased unscrupulous)   (mean immoral aloft)

Each letter stands for a number. Work out the answer to each sum as a letter. Write your answer on the line.

Example: A = 1 B = 2 C = 6 D = 12 E = 10   D ÷ B = (__C__)

10. A = 6   B = 8   C = 13   D = 18   E = 26   E – D = (_____)

11. A = 2   B = 3   C = 6   D = 18   E = 19   D ÷ B – B = (_____)

12. A = 6   B = 7   C = 8   D = 9   E = 10   B + D – E = (_____)

13. A = 2   B = 3   C = 4   D = 6   E = 8   E ÷ A × B – D = (_____)

The number codes for three of these four words are listed in a random order. Work out the code to answer the questions.

LANE   NAIL   NEAR   EARL

4261   3251   1234

14. Find the code for the word **NEAR**.   (_____)

15. Find the code for the word **LAIR**.   (_____)

16. Find the word that has the number code **2642**. (_____)

END OF TEST

/ 16

You have **10 minutes** to do this test. Work as quickly and accurately as you can.

Choose the word that has a similar meaning to the words in both sets of brackets. Underline your answer.

Example: (twig   branch)   (fasten   attach)   glue   <u>stick</u>   trunk   affix   bough

---

1. (boulder stone)   (sway swing)   pebble shake move rock

2. (rearrange mix)   (shamble straggle)   stumble reorder shuffle jumble

3. (establish start)   (discovered located)   found initiate spotted form

4. (ravine canyon)   (overeat overindulge)   pass gulf devour gorge

---

Underline the pair of letters that completes each sentence in the most sensible way. Use the alphabet to help you.

A B C D E F G H I J K L M N O P Q R S T U V W X Y Z

Example: DG is to FE as RU is to (<u>TS</u> SR TU ST US).

---

5. **RZ** is to **OU** as **TP** is to (QL   QK   PL   RK   RJ).

6. **DB** is to **BD** as **LT** is to (IV   JU   KW   KV   JV).

7. **AH** is to **IM** as **FC** is to (NH   OH   MG   OI   NI).

8. **VG** is to **RM** as **WI** is to (SP   RN   TO   TP   SO).

Underline a word from the first set, followed by a word from the second set, that go together to form a new word.

Example: (<u>water</u> suggest disc) (<u>fall</u> hard ton) (The word is **waterfall**.)

9. (heart news toads)   (stool burn sprint)

10. (yours pins broad)   (band self stripe)

11. (them counter heart)   (ten me part)

12. (pass rest overt)   (rain sword turn)

Find the pair of letters that continues each sequence in the best way. Use the alphabet to help you.

A B C D E F G H I J K L M N O P Q R S T U V W X Y Z

Example: TU   QR   NO   KL   HI   (<u>EF</u>)

13. SX   QU   OR   MO KL   (_____)

14. RM   NQ   MN   IR   HO   (_____)

15. CY   ET   FO   HJ   IE   (_____)

16. OL   LN   KQ   HS   GV   (_____)

END OF TEST

/ 16

This puzzle page is full of riddles to test your **logic** skills. Let's see how you do.

A Shock for Mr Poole

Mr Poole leads the chess club at Clever Clogs School. Haji, Miranda, Tarquin and Rufus attend every week. One day, the pupils decided to try and make Mr Poole jump while he was preparing the chessboards in the classroom. Each pupil entered the classroom separately, but only one pupil managed to scare him.

Use the clues and the grid below to work out who made Mr Poole jump.

- Haji didn't have a spider or a wind-up mouse.

- Miranda put on a monster mask.

- Rufus didn't come armed with a spider, which is what made Mr Poole jump.

	Haji	Miranda	Tarquin	Rufus
rubber snake				
spider				
monster mask				
wind-up mouse				

The pupil who made Mr Poole jump was _____.

What Letter am I?

a. If you take me out of a bridge, you'll find me at a wedding.

What letter am I? _____

b. If you take me out of a marker, you'll find a creator.

What letter am I? _____

c. If you take me out of a duvet, you'll find a song.

What letter am I? _____

You have **10 minutes** to do this test. Work as quickly and accurately as you can.

In each sentence below, a four-letter word is hidden at the end of one word and the start of the next. Write the hidden word on the line.

Example: We were flying <u>low</u> below the clouds.   (<u>glow</u>)

---

1.   Look at that adder hiding under the rock!   (_____)

2.   Daisy saw the admiral on the deck.   (_____)

3.   There was a ghost under my bed.   (_____)

4.   We often play catch in the garden.   (_____)

Three of the words in each list are linked. Underline the two words that are **not** related to these three.

Example: puppy   kitten   <u>duck</u>   calf   <u>sheep</u>

---

5.   carry   vehicle   transport   trolley   move

6.   support   back   base   comfort   endorse

7.   chair   director   leader   seat   hall

8.   instruct   enquire   query   command   insist

Find the letter that will finish the first word and start the second word of each pair. The same letter must be used for both pairs.

Example: par (?) een   bac (?) ept   (__k__)

9. bea (?) ear   cur (?) ark   (_____)

10. tal (?) ite   dis (?) ore   (_____)

11. brea (?) eal   drea (?) eem   (_____)

12. brin (?) ill   sin (?) rate   (_____)

Read the information carefully, then use it to answer the question that follows.

13. Alex, Barley, Carrie, Etienne and Gisela are sewing. Gisela sews the highest number of stitches per minute. Alex sews 15 stitches per minute. Barley sews twice as many stitches as Carrie per minute. Carrie and Etienne do the same amount of stitches per minute.

If the statements above are true, only one of the sentences below **must** be true. Which one? Circle the correct letter.

A   Carrie and Etienne are the fastest stitchers.

B   Carrie and Etienne are the slowest stitchers.

C   Barley is not the slowest stitcher.

D   Barley is the fastest stitcher.

E   Alex is the slowest stitcher.

14. Joe, Mary, Briana, Lewis and Olga all have a part in the school play. There are five roles in total, and each role appears on stage at a different time. Briana plays a star, and is the first to appear on stage at 18.07. Briana is on stage by herself for four minutes before Olga joins her. The donkey is the last to appear on stage at 18.21. Joe plays a tree, and walks on to the stage after Olga and four minutes before the donkey. Neither Mary nor Lewis play the snowflake. Mary isn't the donkey, and she appears on stage two minutes after the tree.

If the statements above are true, only one of the sentences below **cannot** be true. Which one? Circle the correct letter.

A   Olga appears on stage six minutes before the tree.

B   The play lasts a total of 14 minutes.

C   The angel, which appears on stage at 18.19, is Lewis's role.

D   The snowflake appears on stage at 18.11.

E   Mary is on stage for the longest period of time.

END OF TEST

/ 14

You have **10 minutes** to do this test. Work as quickly and accurately as you can.

Choose two words, one from each set of brackets, that complete the sentence in the most sensible way. Underline both words.

Example: **Library** is to (book <u>read</u> quietly) as **bakery** is to (baker tasty <u>bake</u>).

1. **Sketch** is to (lines draw coloured) as **draft** is to (pen published write).

2. **Wash** is to (clothes dirt soap) as **iron** is to (crease steam appliance).

3. **Teeth** are to (chatter clamp grind) as **body** is to (cool shiver shake).

4. **Scratch** is to (itch tickle irritate) as **drink** is to (liquid quench thirst).

Each question uses a different code. Use the alphabet to help you work out the answer to each question.

A B C D E F G H I J K L M N O P Q R S T U V W X Y Z

Example: If the code for **MANY** is **LZMX**, what is the code for **GREY**? (<u>FQDX</u>)

5. If the code for **GERM** is **JHUP**, what is the code for **BOAT**? (_____)

6. If the code for **FISH** is **GKVL**, what is **HQDX** the code for? (_____)

7. If the code for **CORD** is **XLIW**, what is the code for **HAIL**? (_____)

8. If the code for **GRAB** is **IVGJ**, what is **UETL** the code for? (_____)

70

The words in the second set follow the same pattern as the words in the first set. Find the missing word to complete the second set. Write the answer on the line.

Example: gate (tie) lid   boat (__art__) arm

9. cram (make) joke   bran (_____) soil

10. bark (rake) kite   pass (_____) male

11. sold (dose) bone   lisp (_____) sell

12. call (coal) oats   sign (_____) once

Find the pair of letters that continues each sequence in the best way. Use the alphabet to help you.

A B C D E F G H I J K L M N O P Q R S T U V W X Y Z

Example: TU   QR   NO   KL   HI   (__EF__)

13. FB   EC   DD   CE   BF   (_____)

14. ZX   WV   TT   QR   NP   (_____)

15. LY   OT   SV   XQ   DS   (_____)

16. DQ   FP   JN   LK   PG   (_____)

END OF TEST

/ 16

You have **10 minutes** to do this test. Work as quickly and accurately as you can.

> Find the letter that will finish the first word and start the second word of each pair. The same letter must be used for both pairs.
>
> **Example:** par (?) een   bac (?) ept   (__k__)

1. plo (?) oll   moul (?) oubt   (_____)

2. bel (?) ight   cul (?) all   (_____)

3. sol (?) ast   min (?) ase   (_____)

4. sla (?) ale   lam (?) arn   (_____)

> The number codes for three of these four words are listed in a random order. Work out the code to answer the questions.

EMIT   TIME   MILE   VEIL

6435   4132   1354

5. Find the code for the word **TIME**.   (_____)

6. Find the code for the word **LIVE**.   (_____)

7. Find the word that has the number code **1324**. (_____)

Underline two words, one from each set of brackets, that have the most opposite meaning.

Example: (eager <u>happy</u> curious)   (tired <u>sad</u> unwell)

8. (demanding thorough precise) (inexact sparse neglected)

9. (pacify quell deaden)   (burden perturb bore)

10. (thicken extend prosper)   (fade languish extinguish)

11. (slack loose disconnect)   (join equal combination)

Each letter stands for a number. Work out the answer to each sum as a letter. Write your answer on the line.

Example: $A = 1$ $B = 2$ $C = 6$ $D = 12$ $E = 10$ $D \div B = (\underline{\quad C \quad})$

12. $A = 4$ $B = 5$ $C = 7$ $D = 10$ $E = 12$ $C + D - E = (\underline{\qquad})$

13. $A = 1$ $B = 2$ $C = 3$ $D = 6$ $E = 12$ $A \times B \times C = (\underline{\qquad})$

14. $A = 1$ $B = 2$ $C = 3$ $D = 4$ $E = 5$ $A \times D - C = (\underline{\qquad})$

15. $A = 4$ $B = 5$ $C = 16$ $D = 18$ $E = 20$ $C \div A \times B - A = (\underline{\qquad})$

16. $A = 3$ $B = 7$ $C = 8$ $D = 12$ $E = 20$ $D \div A \times B - E = (\underline{\qquad})$

END OF TEST

/ 16

Test 29

You have **10 minutes** to do this test. Work as quickly and accurately as you can.

Find the three-letter word that completes the word in capital letters, and so finishes the sentence in a sensible way. Write your answer on the line.

Example: It can be **CHY** outside when it snows.   (_ILL_)

---

1. Sophie dipped the lolly in the **SBET**.   (_____)

2. They wrote in their travel **JNALS** daily.   (_____)

3. He deftly **ESED** through the window.   (_____)

4. Have you **SLD** that cheese yet?   (_____)

Find the number that continues each sequence in the best way. Write your answer on the line.

Example: 3   6   9   12   15 (_18_)

---

5.   9   10   12   15   19   (_____)

6.   3   4   7   11   18   (_____)

7.   48   6   24   12   12   24   (_____)

8.   5   73   10   64   20   55   (_____)

Underline two words, one from each set of brackets, that have the most opposite meaning.

Example: (eager <u>happy</u> curious)   (tired <u>sad</u> unwell)

9. (show present demonstrate)   (performance debut theatre)

10. (apprehend detain release)   (sentence seize forfeit)

11. (accost aggravate insult)   (overburden spurn confront)

12. (fiend sly deceive)   (cunning stealthily immoral)

Each question uses a different code. Use the alphabet to help you work out the answer to each question.

A B C D E F G H I J K L M N O P Q R S T U V W X Y Z

Example: If the code for **MANY** is **LZMX**, what is the code for **GREY**? (<u>FQDX</u>)

13. If the code for **PALE** is **SDOH**, what is the code for **BIRD**?   (_____)

14. If the code for **FADE** is **GCGI**, what is **CQOX** the code for?   (_____)

15. If the code for **MAIL** is **OYKJ**, what is the code for **TIME**?   (_____)

16. If the code for **GOAL** is **TLZO**, what is **HSRK** the code for?   (_____)

END OF TEST

/ 16

Puzzles 8

Take a break! These fun puzzles let you practise your **word** and **number** skills.

Ski Lift

Change one letter at a time to make the first word in each ladder the final word. The two missing words must be real words. When you have filled in the ladders, unscramble the shaded letters to find a hidden word.

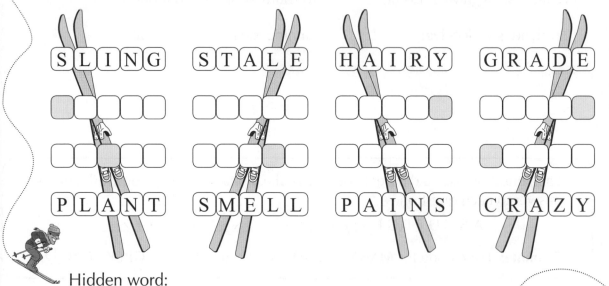

S L I N G STALE HAIRY GRADE

P L A N T SMELL PAINS CRAZY

Hidden word: _ _ _ _ _ _ _

Ski Race

Seven skiers are taking part in a four-event ski competition. They each start their events at a different time. The chart below shows their start times. Work out Jones's start time for each race, based on the pattern of the timings of the skiers that come before her.

Race	Roux	Allegro	Smith	Valls	Klasson	Böhm	Jones
Slalom	11.01	11.03	11.05	11.07	11.09	11.11	
Freestyle	13.21	13.22	13.24	13.27	13.31	13.36	
Downhill	15.45	15.46	15.49	15.54	16.01	16.10	
Ski jump	17.28	17.29	17.31	17.34	17.39	17.47	

10

You have **10 minutes** to do this test. Work as quickly and accurately as you can.

Underline a word from the first set, followed by a word from the second set, that go together to form a new word.

Example: (<u>water</u> suggest disc)   (<u>fall</u> hard ton)   (The word is **waterfall**.)

1.   (sand hum form)   (mat bag all)

2.   (budge for overt)   (get cast head)

3.   (sculpt found cult)   (your or are)

4.   (car tang rib)   (bone age go)

Choose the word that has a similar meaning to the words in both sets of brackets. Underline your answer.

Example: (twig   branch) (fasten   attach)   glue <u>stick</u> trunk affix bough

5.   (transport move)   (boat ferry)   load ship lift freight

6.   (council ministry)   (cupboard dresser)   chest advisory team cabinet

7.   (crushed powdered)   (floor earth)   soil ground base grated

8.   (vex irk)   (foil thwart)   madden defeat frustrate annoy

9. Iago, Gabe, Alexei, Anouk and Elspeth are counting the pens in their pencil case. Iago has 4 pens. Gabe has 12 pens, but gives 2 to Alexei. Alexei has the fewest pens. Anouk has the second highest number of pens. Gabe has more pens than Anouk. Elspeth has as many pens as Iago and Alexei combined.

    If the statements above are true, only one of the sentences below **must** be true. Which one? Circle the correct letter.

    A Iago has the fourth highest number of pens.

    B Gabe has the largest pencil case.

    C Elspeth has the highest number of pens.

    D Gabe has the third highest number of pens.

    E Elspeth has more pens than Anouk.

10. A right-hand drive minibus has room for eight passengers, including the driver. The seats are arranged in four rows. Six seats are currently occupied. Avril and Brian are sat in the last two seats. Konnie is sat two seats in front of Avril, directly behind the driver. Dan's seat is diagonally opposite Brian's. Eli is sat next to Dan.

    If the statements above are true, only one of the sentences below must be true. Which one? Circle the correct letter.

    A Two seats separate Konnie from Dan.

    B Eli is sat in the third row from the front.

    C Brian is sat on the same side of the bus as Konnie.

    D The seat next to the driver is occupied.

    E Avril is sat within reaching distance of Eli.

Find the number that completes the final set of numbers in the same way as the first two sets. Write your answer on the line.

Example: 7 (4) 3   10 (5) 5   15 (__11__) 4

11. 6 (11) 4   3 (16) 12   5 (_____) 11

12. 6 (4) 2   10 (14) 18   11 (_____) 7

13. 2 (6) 10   3 (3) 6   4 (_____) 12

14. 4 (5) 3   6 (8) 4   7 (_____) 1

END OF TEST

/ 14

You have **10 minutes** to do this test. Work as quickly and accurately as you can.

> In each sentence below, a four-letter word is hidden at the end of one word and the start of the next. Write the hidden word on the line.
>
> **Example:** We were flying <u>low</u> below the clouds.   (<u>glow</u>)

1. James said he didn't want to come.   (_____)

2. Can I help open all these?   (_____)

3. Where are you going to go now?   (_____)

4. She updated us about all the family.   (_____)

5. Are you too busy to look after me?   (_____)

> Find the number that continues each sequence in the best way. Write your answer on the line.
>
> **Example:** 3   6   9   12   15 (__18__)

6. 5   9   14   20   27   (_____)

7. 2   3   5   8   13   21   (_____)

8. 22   20   20   22   26   32 (_____)

9. 12   2   16   4   20   8   (_____)

Choose two words, one from each set of brackets, that complete the sentence in the most sensible way. Underline both words.

Example: **Library** is to (book <u>read</u> quietly) as **bakery** is to (baker tasty <u>bake</u>).

10. **Stage** is to (audience curtain theatre) as **screen** is to (actor cinema advert).

11. **Carpenter** is to (wood saw tree) as **painter** is to (gloss coat paintbrush).

12. **Dictionary** is to (define meaning word) as **calculator** is to (count calculate maths).

13. **Solution** is to (blend solve problem) as **discovery** is to (scientist unexpected find).

The number codes for three of these four words are listed in a random order. Work out the code to answer the questions.

SHOP   POSH   STOP   HOSE

3521   1234   4236

14. Find the code for the word **SHOP**.   (_____)

15. Find the code for the word **SPOT**.   (_____)

16. Find the word that has the number code **3426**. (_____)

END OF TEST

/ 16

(10)

You have **10 minutes** to do this test. Work as quickly and accurately as you can.

Remove one letter from the first word and add it to the second word to make two new words. Do not change the order of the other letters. Write the letter that moves on the line.

Example: claw   age   (___C___)   (The new words are **law** and **cage**.)

1. bland   are   (_____)

2. place   gum   (_____)

3. rifle   eel   (_____)

4. mince   hut   (_____)

Find the number that completes the final set of numbers in the same way as the first two sets. Write your answer on the line.

Example: 7 (4) 3   10 (5) 5   15 (__11__) 4

5.   6 (3) 3   10 (6) 2   12 (_____) 4

6.   4 (12) 6   6 (21) 7   4 (_____) 8

7.   12 (2) 5   18 (10) 4   20 (_____) 3

8.   20 (4) 8   19 (6) 1   39 (_____) 9

Three of the words in each list are linked. Underline the two words that are **not** related to these three.

Example: puppy   kitten   <u>duck</u>   calf   <u>sheep</u>

9. plum   raisin   peach   prune   cherry

10. throw   slide   launch   hurl   roll

11. confirm   propose   suggest   certify   approve

12. old   elderly   mature   ancient   senior

Each question uses a different code. Use the alphabet to help you work out the answer to each question.

A B C D E F G H I J K L M N O P Q R S T U V W X Y Z

Example: If the code for **MANY** is **LZMX**, what is the code for **GREY**? (<u>FQDX</u>)

13. If the code for **BARK** is **EDUN**, what is the code for **OPEN**?   (_____)

14. If the code for **SIGN** is **TKJR**, what is **CGDV** the code for?   (_____)

15. If the code for **TICK** is **OEZI**, what is the code for **BLUE**?   (_____)

16. If the code for **LEAF** is **OVZU**, what is **XLIW** the code for?   (_____)

END OF TEST

/ 16

You have **10 minutes** to do this test. Work as quickly and accurately as you can.

> The words in the second set follow the same pattern as the words in the first set. Find the missing word to complete the second set. Write the answer on the line.
>
> **Example:** gate (tie) lid   boat (__art__) arm

1. break (dear) dog   steam (_____) bid

2. stall (ball) grub   dwelt (_____) turf

3. light (girl) rule   spell (_____) itch

4. dark (raid) ride   told (_____) afar

> Each letter stands for a number. Work out the answer to each sum as a letter. Write your answer on the line.
>
> **Example:** A = 1 B = 2 C = 6 D = 12 E = 10   D ÷ B = (___C___)

5. A = 2 B = 3   C = 4   D = 7   E = 8   E – C + B = (_____)

6. A = 2 B = 11 C = 12 D = 24 E = 34   B × A + C = (_____)

7. A = 1 B = 2   C = 3   D = 5   E = 10   E ÷ D + B – A = (_____)

8. A = 3 B = 10 C = 20 D = 30 E = 60   E ÷ A + B – C = (_____)

Find the number that continues each sequence in the best way. Write your answer on the line.

Example: 3 6 9 12 15 (__18__)

9. 21 16 12 9 7   (_____)

10. 2 3 7 16 32   (_____)

11. 1 9 3 5 5 1   (_____)

12. 2 14 4 17 8 20   (_____)

Underline the pair of letters that completes each sentence in the most sensible way. Use the alphabet to help you.

A B C D E F G H I J K L M N O P Q R S T U V W X Y Z

Example: **DG** is to **FE** as **RU** is to (<u>TS</u> SR TU ST US).

13. **GJ** is to **KO** as **PT** is to   (TX   SX   TY   TZ   SY).

14. **JW** is to **MQ** as **GA** is to (KV   JU   KU   JT   JV).

15. **NG** is to **ML** as **PK** is to (OO   PO   QO   NP   OP).

16. **YN** is to **BM** as **VS** is to (EH   EG   DG   DF   DH).

END OF TEST

/ 16

Test 34

Time for a break! These puzzles are a great way to practise your **logic** skills.

Word Grid

Use the words below to fill in the blanks in the word grid. You must use all the words. One letter has been filled in for you.

flamed, dreary, accord, defeat, chance, decide

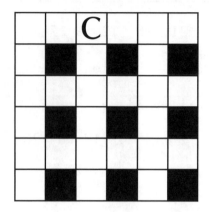

Mysterious Messages

Decode each of the messages below.
Each message has a sample code provided.

A B C D E F G H I J K L M N O P Q R S T U V W X Y Z

a)   BRING — in code: EULQJ   Message: ZKHUH LV WKH FKHHVH?

Message: ....

b)   GREY — in code: CNAU   Message: E DWRA HKOP IU IKQOA.

Message: ....

c)   FROG — in code: UILT   Message: GSV XZG MVVWH Z YZGS.

Message: ....

You have **10 minutes** to do this test. Work as quickly and accurately as you can.

Find the word that completes the third pair of words so that it follows the same pattern as the first two pairs. Write your answer on the line.

Example: boat oat   chip hip   land (_**and**_)

1.   dollar load   normal moan   topped   (_____)

2.   funded dune   forces sore   packer   (_____)

3.   pine ping   mail main   reed   (_____)

4.   twilit wilt   grinds ring   learnt   (_____)

Find the missing number to complete each sum. Write your answer on the line.

Example: $7 + 5 = 24 \div ($ _**2**_ $)$

5. $14 - 6 = 3 + ($ _____ $)$

6. $15 \times 2 - 8 = 44 \div ($ _____ $)$

7. $21 \div 7 + 9 = 4 \times 5 - ($ _____ $)$

8. $56 \div 8 - 1 = 48 \div 12 + ($ _____ $)$

Underline two words, one from each set of brackets, that have the most opposite meaning.

Example: (eager <u>happy</u> curious)   (tired <u>sad</u> unwell)

9. (past memory recall)   (time revise forget)

10. (modern fresh retro)   (outmoded dilapidated historic)

11. (serious doleful intense)   (relieved gracious exuberant)

12. (suppress unnerve aggravate) (alleviate deactivate quieten)

Read the information carefully, then use it to answer the question that follows.

13. Lola, Peapod, Lara, Sophie and Charlie are cats. Peapod has the lowest number of stripes. Lara doesn't have the third highest number of stripes. Lola has more stripes than Sophie. Sophie has the second highest number of stripes.

If the statements above are true, only one of the sentences below **must** be true. Which one? Circle the correct letter.

A   Charlie has twice as many stripes as Lara.

B   Lola has the highest number of stripes.

C   Charlie has more stripes than Lola.

D   Charlie has the fourth highest number of stripes.

E   Lara has the lowest number of stripes.

14. A group of children who only spoke English were taught to say 'hello' in German, French, Italian, Spanish and Russian. Before they learnt to say 'hello' in Russian, they could already say 'hello' in three languages. After they learnt how to say 'hello' in Spanish, they could say 'hello' in five languages. They did not learn German last. Italian was neither the last nor the second language the pupils learnt.

If the statements above are true, only one of the sentences below **must** be true. Which one? Circle the correct letter.

A   During the lesson, the pupils were taught to say 'hello' in six languages.

B   The pupils learnt some German after they had learnt some Russian.

C   After the Spanish lesson, the pupils had learnt to say 'hello' in Spanish, French and Russian.

D   Spanish was the fourth language the pupils learnt.

E   Just before they learnt some Russian, the pupils were able to say 'hello' in Spanish.

END OF TEST

/ 14

You have **10 minutes** to do this test. Work as quickly and accurately as you can.

Underline two words, one from each set of brackets, that have the most opposite meaning.

Example: (eager <u>happy</u> curious)   (tired <u>sad</u> unwell)

---

1. (employer cheque colleague)   (wage co-worker teamwork)

2. (accord resemblance relevance)   (similarity match alignment)

3. (disassemble upturn ransack)   (deface storm scour)

4. (antagonistic futile disrespectful)   (disloyal negative hostile)

Each letter stands for a number. Work out the answer to each sum as a letter. Write your answer on the line.

Example: A = 1 B = 2 C = 6 D = 12 E = 10 $D \div B = ($ <u>   C   </u> $)$

---

5.   A = 6   B = 8   C = 9   D = 18   E = 27 $D - C = ($ _____ $)$

6.   A = 6   B = 7   C = 8   D = 48   E = 56 $A \times C = ($ _____ $)$

7.   A = 1   B = 3   C = 4   D = 10   E = 11 $C \times B - E = ($ _____ $)$

8.   A = 4   B = 5   C = 6   D = 8   E = 10 $D \div A + C = ($ _____ $)$

In each sentence below, a four-letter word is hidden at the end of one word and the start of the next. Write the hidden word on the line.

Example: We were flying <u>low</u> below the clouds. (<u>glow</u>)

9. The church appointed a charismatic leader. (_____)

10. Officials built the sixth arena in Mexico. (_____)

11. Plum pudding tastes great alongside whipped cream. (_____)

12. The spy knew too much about them. (_____)

Each question uses a different code. Use the alphabet to help you work out the answer to each question.

A B C D E F G H I J K L M N O P Q R S T U V W X Y Z

Example: If the code for **MANY** is **LZMX**, what is the code for **GREY**? (<u>FQDX</u>)

13. If the code for **JOKE** is **INJD**, what is the code for **LAST**? (_____)

14. If the code for **IRON** is **JTPP**, what is **NGBN** the code for? (_____)

15. If the code for **SACK** is **UEIS**, what is the code for **GONG**? (_____)

16. If the code for **PLAY** is **SHDU**, what is **UKDZ** the code for? (_____)

END OF TEST

/ 16

Test 36

You have **10 minutes** to do this test. Work as quickly and accurately as you can.

Three of the words in each list are linked. Underline the two words that are **not** related to these three.

Example: puppy   kitten   <u>duck</u>   calf   <u>sheep</u>

1. glove   shoe   slipper   blouse   sock

2. lights   mistletoe   bauble   holly   tinsel

3. recover   suffer   cure   treat   operate

4. institution   department   division   company   section

The number codes for three of these four words are listed in a random order. Work out the code to answer the questions.

READ   TALE   AREA   LARD

6146   2615   3624

5. Find the code for the word **READ**.   (_____)

6. Find the code for the word **DART**.   (_____)

7. Find the word that has the number code **5461**. (_____)

The words in the second set follow the same pattern as the words in the first set. Find the missing word to complete the second set. Write the answer on the line.

Example: gate (tie) lid   boat (__art__) arm

8. nose (son) slap   tear (_____) wait

9. fool (oil) clip   face (_____) span

10. team (tap) pity   whit (_____) pint

11. ware (wart) tear   kiln (_____) took

12. oily (boil) bold   hate (_____) feel

Find the missing number to complete each sum. Write your answer on the line.

Example: $7 + 5 = 24 \div ($ __2__ $)$

13. $34 - 6 = 24 + ($ _____ $)$

14. $6 \times 6 - 11 = 50 \div ($ _____ $)$

15. $15 + 6 - 7 = 2 \times ($ _____ $)$

16. $54 \div 9 \times 8 = 12 \times 5 - ($ _____ $)$

END OF TEST

/ 16

This final puzzle page tests your **word making** and **numeracy** skills one last time.

Word Generator

Use the letters on the word generator machine to make as many four letter words as you can in 3 minutes. You can only use each letter once in each word. The words must contain the letter 'D'. Write your words in the box below.

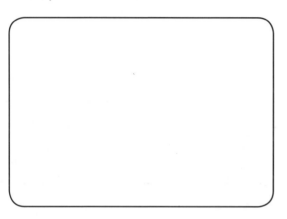

Number Path

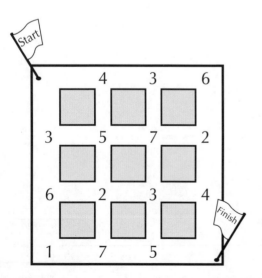

Draw a line from the start to the finish on the grid. The numbers your line passes through should add up to 32.

V6XPE1

CGP

11+

Verbal Reasoning

Ages

10-11

The
Answer Book

Verbal
Reasoning

The 11+
10-Minute Tests

Practise • Prepare • Pass

Everything your child needs for 11+ success

Test 1 — pages 2-3

1. l
The new words are 'hurl', 'lean', 'boil' and 'lawn'.

2. d
The new words are 'raid', 'dial', 'prod' and 'dark'.

3. m
The new words are 'warm', 'more', 'calm' and 'most'.

4. e
The new words are 'care', 'ears', 'isle' and 'earl'.

5. part
'part' can mean 'a person in a play or film' or 'to split in two'.

6. shed
'shed' can mean 'a shack' or 'to take off'.

7. suspend
'suspend' can mean 'to defer' or 'to hang from somewhere'.

8. book
'book' can mean 'to make a reservation' or 'a written or printed work'.

9. 10
$15 + 4 = 19, 19 = 29 - 10$

10. 9
$30 \div 5 + 12 = 18, 18 = 2 \times 9$

11. 11
$7 + 4 - 8 = 3, 3 = 33 \div 11$

12. 9
$12 \div 4 \times 6 = 18, 18 = 2 \times 9$

13. WS
The first letter in the pair moves forward 8 letters, the second letter moves forward 2 letters.

14. JP
The first letter in the pair moves back 4 letters, the second letter moves forward 4 letters.

15. YI
The first letter in the pair moves forward 7 letters, the second letter moves back 4 letters.

16. PK
The first letter in the pair moves forward 6 letters, the second letter moves back 6 letters.

Test 2 — pages 4-5

1. e
The new words are 'glad' and 'pine'.

2. r
The new words are 'heat' and 'trip'.

3. c
The new words are 'lean' and 'crow'.

4. u
The new words are 'fond' and 'aunt'.

5. celebrate   commiserate
'celebrate' means 'to acknowledge a happy event', whereas 'commiserate' means 'to acknowledge a sad event'.

6. chastise   commend
'chastise' means 'to scold', whereas 'commend' means 'to praise'.

7. inconsequential   paramount
'inconsequential' means 'insignificant', whereas 'paramount' means 'important'.

8. demonic   angelic
'demonic' means 'devilish', whereas 'angelic' means 'heavenly'.

9. 2
$8 \times 4 = 32, 32 = 64 \div 2$

10. 6
$100 \div 5 = 20, 20 = 3 \times 6 + 2$

11. 11
$21 \div 7 + 3 = 6, 6 = 66 \div 11$

12. 10
$40 - 30 + 20 = 30, 30 = 3 \times 10$

13. OYTI
To get from the word to the code move the letters in the sequence +2, −2, +2, −2.

14. SSQI
To get from the word to the code move the letters in the sequence −3, +4, −3, +4.

15. RAGE
To get from the code to the word move each letter forward 2.

16. GRID
To get from the code to the word move the letters in the sequence +1, +2, +3, +4.

Puzzles 1 — page 6

Crack the Code to find the Treasure

The numbering starts at the letter 'N' and goes backwards through the alphabet. The completed code looks like this:

A	B	C	D	E	F	G	H	I	J	K	L	M
14	13	12	11	10	9	8	7	6	5	4	3	2

N	O	P	Q	R	S	T	U	V	W	X	Y	Z
1	26	25	24	23	22	21	20	19	18	17	16	15

The treasure is buried under the **lighthouse**.

Find the Hidden Word

The hidden word is **silver** (ba**silver**sus).

Test 3 — pages 7-9

1.   lean
The word is hidden in the phrase 'cycle anticlockwise'.

2.   them
The word is hidden in the phrase 'the mouse'.

3.   pest
The word is hidden in the phrase 'hopes to'.

4.   seat
The word is hidden in the phrase 'those atlases'.

5.   bolt
'bolt' can mean 'leave quickly' or 'seal shut'.

6.   mind
'mind' can mean 'to care for' or 'intelligence'.

7.   bitter
'bitter' can mean a 'tart taste' or 'hostile'.

8.   kind
'kind' can mean 'variety' or 'cordial'.

9.   D
James's cookies were the widest. Rosie's were over 1.1 m, and Rachael's were half this size. We don't know how big Susannah and Amélie's cookies were. That means that we know that Rachael's cookies were not the second widest because both James and Rosie's cookies were bigger. Regardless of whether Susannah and Amélie's cookies were bigger or smaller, Rachael's cookies would still not be the second widest.

10.   A
The first floor has two departments, and gifts are on the top floor. Toys and children's wear are next to each other and therefore must be on the first floor because the ground floor only has one department. Men's wear is not on the ground floor and therefore must be on the top floor. Therefore, women's wear must be on the ground floor, and it cannot be true that the gift department is directly above women's wear.

11.   4
$7 \times 2 = 14, 14 = 10 + 4$

12.   2
$18 \div 3 = 6, 6 = 4 \times 2 - 2$

13.   5
$9 \times 3 + 8 = 35, 35 = 7 \times 5$

14.   3
$5 + 5 + 7 = 17, 17 = 60 \div 3 - 3$

Test 4 — pages 10-11

1.   LOW
The complete word is SWALLOWED.

2.   ICE
The complete word is SLICED.

3.   FUN
The complete word is REFUND.

4.   GET
The complete word is TARGETED.

5.   famine   drought
The other three all mean 'insufficiency'.

6.   victorious   triumphant
The other three are all nouns that mean 'achievement'.

7.   sympathetic   understanding
The other three all mean 'joyful'.

8.   card   letter
The other three are things you need to send a card or letter by post.

9.   atmospheric   ethereal
The other three all mean 'physically attractive'.

10.   24
Add the two outside numbers together.

11.   15
Multiply the two outside numbers together and then divide the answer by 2.

12.   26
Multiply the two outside numbers together and then add 2 to the answer.

13.   20
Square both of the outside numbers, then subtract the squared number on the right from the squared number on the left.

14.   1543
$L = 1, A = 5, T = 4, E = 3$

15.   6354
$S = 6, E = 3, A = 5, T = 4$

16.   TALE
$T = 4, A = 5, L = 1, E = 3$

Test 5 — pages 12-13

1.   time
Take letters 2 and 3 from the first word, followed by letters 1 and 2 from the second word.

2.   some
Take letters 1 and 2 from the first word, followed by letters 1 and 2 from the second word.

3.   lift
Take letters 3 and 2 from the first word, followed by letters 3 and 4 from the second word.

4.   ram
Take letter 2 from the first word, followed by letters 4 and 3 from the second word.

5.   tree   bush
They describe what apples and blackberries grow on.

6.   snow   wind
They are key features of a blizzard and a hurricane.

7.   eat   drink
They are verbs that are associated with the verbs 'nibble' and 'sip'.

3

8. aviation dance
They describe the industries that a pilot and a choreographer work in.

9. D
$3 + 5 + 6 = 14, D = 14$

10. E
$15 \div 3 + 10 = 15, E = 15$

11. B
$32 \div 8 \times 1 = 4, B = 4$

12. E
$24 \div 12 \times 2 + 20 = 24, E = 24$

13. HS
The first letter moves forward 2 letters.
The second letter moves back 2 letters.

14. KP
The first letter moves forward 4 letters.
The second letter moves forward 8 letters.

15. VR
CG and XT are mirror pairs, where the two letters are an equal distance from the centre of the alphabet. The answer will be the mirror pairs for E and I, which are V and R.

16. YV
The first letter moves forward 5 letters.
The second letter moves back 2 letters.

Test 6 — pages 14-15

1. without
'without' is the only correctly spelled word that can be made.

2. handlebar
'handlebar' is the only correctly spelled word that can be made.

3. combat
'combat' is the only correctly spelled word that can be made.

4. perform
'perform' is the only correctly spelled word that can be made.

5. amble stroll
Both words mean 'to walk slowly'.

6. disintegrate crumble
Both words mean 'to fall apart'.

7. relish savour
Both words mean 'to enjoy'.

8. rest relax
Both words mean 'to unwind'.

9. QQ
Both letters move in the sequence +1, +2, +3, +4, +5.

10. WR
The first letter moves in the sequence -1, -2, -3, -4, -5.
The second letter moves in the sequence +1, +2, +3, +4, +5.

11. AS
The first letter moves in the sequence -1, -0, +1, +2, +3.
The second letter moves forward 3 letters each time.

12. MM
The first letter moves forward 2 letters each time. The second letter moves in the sequence +1, +1, +2, +3, +5, where the two previous increments are added together.

13. KHOS
To get from the word to the code, move each letter forward 3.

14. CLIP
To get from the code to the word, move each letter forward 4.

15. UILT
This is a mirror code, where the letters are an equal distance from the centre of the alphabet. U is a mirror of F, I is a mirror of R, L is a mirror of O and T is a mirror of G.

16. POACH
To get from the code to the word, move the letters in the sequence -1, -2, -3, -4, -5.

Puzzles 2 — page 16

Antonym Antics

Spell and Unscramble
You should have crossed out: b, u, n, n, a, c, d, a, e.
Antonym for lack: **abundance**

Test 7 — pages 17-19

1. chat
Rearrange letters 1, 3, 4 and 5 in the order 4, 5, 3, 1.

2. near
Rearrange letters 2, 3, 4 and 5 in the order 5, 2, 3, 4.

3. sale
Remove letters 2, 4 and 7, leaving the remaining letters in the order 1, 3, 5, 6.

4. core
Rearrange letters 1, 3, 4 and 6 in the order 1, 4, 3, 6.

5. superfluous headstrong
They are synonyms of 'redundant' and 'wilful'.

6. supply answer
They are responses to 'demand' and 'question'.

7. dispose digest
They describe what happens to waste and food.

8. reward illusion

They are synonyms of 'bounty' and 'mirage'.

9. E

The pool is 3 metres deep, which is 300 cm. Becki missed the bottom of the pool by 140 cm, so she dived 160 cm. Aadi reached the bottom, so Aadi dived 300 cm. Catherine dived half as deep as Aadi, so Catherine dived 150 cm. The passage says "Neither Di nor Ed had the shallowest dive." Therefore, Catherine had the shallowest dive.

10. B

We know that the castle is in square C4. The tower is two squares south of the castle, so it must be in square C2. The dungeon is one square west of the tower, so it must be in square B2. The forest is three squares north-east of the dungeon, so it must be in square E5. The sand dunes are one square away from the castle and three squares away from the dungeon, so it must be in square B5. Square B5 is three squares west of E5, so the sand dunes must be three squares west of the forest.

11. 2

Divide the first number by the third number.

12. 33

Add the two outer numbers together, then subtract 2.

13. 26

Subtract the third number from the first number, then multiply by 2.

14. 10

Divide the first number by the third number, then add 4.

Test 8 — pages 20-21

1. tea

Take letter 3 from the second word, followed by letters 2 and 3 from the first word.

2. art

Take letters 2 and 3 from the first word, followed by letter 3 from the second word.

3. dam

Take letters 1 and 3 from the first word, followed by letter 3 from the second word.

4. lid

Take letters 3 and 2 from the first word, followed by letter 4 from the second word.

5. 1264

$P = 1, O = 2, R = 6, T = 4$

6. 4651

$T = 4, R = 6, A = 5, P = 1$

7. RATE

$R = 6, 5 = A, T = 4, E = 3$

8. dear

'dear' can mean 'to cost a lot' or 'regarded with affection'.

9. custom

'custom' can mean 'the dealings with a business by customers' or 'an accepted way of behaving'.

10. fast

'fast' can mean 'moving at a high speed' or 'immovable'.

11. screen

'screen' can mean 'a flat panel on an electrical device' or 'to check for disease'.

12. D

$5 \times 3 + 5 = 20, D = 20$

13. E

$3 \times 8 - 7 = 17, E = 17$

14. B

$8 + 2 - 5 = 5, B = 5$

15. A

$15 \div 3 + 5 - 7 = 3, A = 3$

16. E

$9 \div 3 \times 2 + 6 = 12, E = 12$

Test 9 — pages 22-23

1. a

The new words are 'chin' and 'road'.

2. e

The new words are 'last' and 'bide'.

3. c

The new words are 'mine' and 'clot'.

4. e

The new words are 'plan' and 'woke'.

5. energize tire

'energize' means 'to enliven', whereas 'tire' means 'to weary'.

6. dishevel groom

'dishevel' means 'to make someone untidy', whereas 'groom' means 'to make someone tidy'.

7. extinguish ignite

'extinguish' means 'to stop burning', whereas 'ignite' means 'to catch fire'.

8. altruistic egocentric

'altruistic' means 'unselfish', whereas 'egocentric' means 'selfish'.

9. gain

Rearrange letters 2, 4, 5 and 6 in the order 6, 2, 4, 5.

10. rely

Rearrange letters 2, 3, 5 and 6 in the order 5, 2, 3, 6.

11. rail

Rearrange letters 2, 3, 4 and 6 in the order 6, 2, 3, 4.

12. clue

The first letter of the word moves forward one place along the alphabet.

13. 4

Subtract 6 each time.

14. 1

Divide by 3 each time.

5

15. 23

The number added increases by 1
each time: +1, +2, +3, +4, +5.

16. 18

There are two sequences which alternate.
In the first sequence, add 4 each time.
In the second, subtract 4 each time.

Test 10 — pages 24-25

1. horseradish

'horseradish' is the only correctly
spelled word that can be made.

2. solid

'solid' is the only correctly spelled word that can be made.

3. limelight

'limelight' is the only correctly spelled
word that can be made.

4. novice

'novice' is the only correctly spelled
word that can be made.

5. wholesome

'wholesome' is the only correctly
spelled word that can be made.

6. lean

'lean' can mean 'tilt' or 'slim'.

7. case

'case' can mean 'an occasion' or 'a
holder to protect something'.

8. noted

'noted' can mean 'well known' or 'put down in writing'.

9. neat

'neat' can mean 'not mixed with anything' or 'well kept'.

10. 25

Add the two outside numbers together and then add 2.

11. 96

Multiply the outside numbers.

12. 1

Divide the first number by the second
number and then subtract 1.

13. 8

Divide the first number by the second number
and then add the second number.

14. 1425

G = 1, R = 4, I = 2, D = 5

15. 5643

D = 5, A = 6, R = 4, E = 3

16. DIRE

D = 5, I = 2, R = 4, E = 3

Puzzles 3 — page 26

Find the Secret Message

1.   gold   midnight

The sentence should read 'The robbers broke
in at midnight and stole the queen's gold.'

2.   delivered   will

The sentence should read 'Hopefully the order
will be delivered on Tuesday morning.'

3.   At   the

The sentence should read 'The clown at
Jane's party was very funny.'

4.   be   medallions

The sentence should read 'Mum's pork medallions will
eventually be ready to eat.'

The secret message is '**The gold medallions
will be delivered at midnight.**'

Wordy Wisdom

a. forty   b. sorty   c. sporty

The sentence should read '**Harry isn't very sporty.**'

Test 11 — pages 27-29

1.   p

The new words are 'clasp', 'plug', 'stop' and 'peer'.

2.   k

The new words are 'book', 'kind', 'bank' and 'king'.

3.   b

The new words are 'herb', 'bark', 'comb' and 'bear'.

4.   l

The new words are 'feel', 'lime', 'curl' and 'lard'.

5.   hoard   stockpile

Both words mean 'a large supply'.

6.   ramble   babble

Both words mean 'to talk or write at
length in a confused manner'.

7.   saunter   wander

Both words mean 'to walk slowly'.

8.   eject   expel

Both words mean 'to force to leave'.

9.   D

From the information, we know that the following
keys work: A, C, D, E, G, K, L, P, R, S, T and U. We
also know that 'I','N' and 'O' don't work. We can
only suspect that 'H' doesn't work. So, D is
the only statement that cannot be true.

10. B

Ailsa's worm is 21 cm long. Corinne's worm is double 21
cm, so her worm is 42 cm long. Isobel's worm is one-third
of 21 cm, so Isobel's worm is 7 cm long. Elgar's worm is
21 cm plus 7 cm, so Elgar's worm is 28 cm long.
The passage says "Isobel's worm is not the shortest."
Therefore, Gajra's worm is the shortest.

11. somewhere
'somewhere' is the only correctly spelled word that can be made.

12. popcorn
'popcorn' is the only correctly spelled word that can be made.

13. styled
'styled' is the only correctly spelled word that can be made.

14. reinforce
'reinforce' is the only correctly spelled word that can be made.

Test 12 — pages 30-31

1. LM
The first letter moves forward 2 letters then 0 letters alternately. The second letter moves in the sequence +2, −1, +2, −1, +2.

2. RC
The first letter moves in the sequence +1, +2, +3, +4, +5. The second letter moves back in the sequence −1, −2, −3, −4, −5.

3. ES
The first letter moves in the sequence +2, +4, +6, +8, +10. The second letter moves forward 2 letters.

4. QX
The first letter moves forward 3 letters. The second letter moves back 1 letter.

5. OT
Each letter in the pair moves forward 3 letters.

6. HR
The first letter in the pair moves forward 1 letter. The second letter moves back 3 letters.

7. SV
The first letter in the pair moves forward 5 letters. The second letter moves forward 6 letters.

8. WS
BF and YU are mirror pairs, where the two letters are an equal distance from the centre of the alphabet. W is the mirror of D and S is the mirror of H.

9. ASK
The complete word is BASKET.

10. SUM
The complete word is CONSUMED.

11. RED
The complete word is CREDIT.

12. HER
The complete word is ADHERE.

13. biscuit   apple
The other three are all liquids.

14. write   compose
The other three are what people do to make pictures.

15. grate   chop
The other three describe how something may be cooked.

16. dive   paddle
The other three are movements that take place in the air.

Test 13 — pages 32-33

1. t
The new words are 'but', 'tore', 'wet' and 'try'.

2. t
The new words are 'cart', 'trim', 'cut' and 'tame'.

3. n
The new words are 'loan', 'near', 'bun' and 'nail'.

4. p
The new words are 'pip', 'pen', 'pup' and 'pain'.

5. WM
The first letter moves in the sequence +1, +2, +3, +4, +5. The second letter moves forward 5 letters each time.

6. PW
The first letter moves forward 3 letters each time. The second letter moves back 3 letters then forward 2 letters alternately.

7. WB
The first letter moves back 1 letter then back 2 letters alternately. The second letter moves forward 4 letters each time.

8. VT
The first letter moves back 1 letter then back 3 letters alternately. The second letter moves forward 3 letters then forward 2 letters alternately.

9. dig
Rearrange letters 1, 2 and 4 in the order 4, 2 and 1.

10. tang
The first letter of the word moves forward one place along the alphabet.

11. prop
Rearrange the letters 1, 3, 4 and 6 in the order 4, 6, 3 and 1.

12. bard
Rearrange the letters 1, 3, 5 and 6 in the order 1, 5, 3 and 6.

13. finish   begin
They are synonyms of 'complete' and 'start'.

14. courage   fear
They are nouns with which the adjectives 'brave' and 'scared' are associated.

15. transparent   opaque
They describe the qualities of a window and a blackboard.

16. brake   accelerate
They are synonyms of 'stop' and 'go'.

Test 14 — pages 34-35

1. 25
Add numbers in ascending order: +1, +2, +3, +4, +5, +6.

2.   64
Add odd numbers in ascending order:
+7, +9, +11, +13, +15.

3.   92
Add square numbers in ascending
order: +4, +9, +16, +25, +36.

4.   28
There are two sequences which alternate.
In the first sequence, subtract 1 each time.
In the second sequence, add 2 each time.

5.   1234
R = 1, E = 2, A = 3, D = 4

6.   4661
D = 4, O = 6, O = 6, R = 1

7.   RATE
R = 1, A = 3, T = 5, E = 2

8.   hear
The word is hidden in the phrase 'the arch'.

9.   army
The word is hidden in the phrase 'shear my'.

10.   yowl
The word is hidden in the phrase 'many owls'.

11.   dart
The word is hidden in the phrase 'had artefacts'.

12.   disallow   accept
'disallow' means 'to reject', whereas 'accept' means
'to permit'.

13.   break   repair
'break' means 'to stop working', whereas
'repair' means 'to make work'.

14.   ornate   plain
'ornate' means 'highly decorative',
whereas 'plain' means 'simple'.

15.   enormous   miniscule
'enormous' means 'very large', whereas
'miniscule' means 'very small'.

16.   idle   active
'idle' means 'lazy', whereas 'active' means 'energetic'.

Puzzles 4 — page 36

Synonym Snake

Crack the Code

JUPITER
Turn the page so it is horizontal, then add one line
to each symbol to make the letters J U P I T E R.

Test 15 — pages 37-39

1.   k
The new words are 'chin' and 'know'.

2.   c
The new words are 'wine' and 'chip'.

3.   o
The new words are 'both' and 'hoop'.

4.   e
The new words are 'wave' and 'poet'.

5.   harbour
'harbour' can mean 'a place to moor ships' or 'to conceal'.

6.   box
'box' can mean 'to strike with one's fists'
or 'a place to store things'.

7.   refuse
'refuse' can mean 'material thrown away' or 'to turn down'.

8.   delegate
'delegate' can mean 'to give someone a
task to do' or 'a representative'.

9.   77
Multiply the two outer numbers.

10.   16
The answer is the midpoint between
the two outer numbers.

11.   20
Add the two outer numbers together.
Subtract 2 from the answer.

12.   7
Multiply the two outer numbers
together. Divide the answer by 4.

13.   D
Finn likes at least one type of vegetable. Ramon dislikes
all types of vegetable. Therefore, it must be true that
Finn likes more types of vegetable than Ramon.

14.   D
Group 1 has eggs, butter and flour, so it needs
sugar and baking powder to bake the cakes. Group
2 has butter, sugar and baking powder, so it needs
eggs and flour to bake the cakes. If Wayne swaps
his sugar for Neil's eggs, Group 2 will still need
flour. So, it cannot be true that if Wayne swaps his
sugar for Neil's eggs, Group 2 will be able to bake.

Test 16 — pages 40-41

1.   tube   carton
They are what toothpaste and juice
are commonly contained in.

2.   meagre   luxurious
They are synonyms of 'scanty' and 'opulent'.

3.   deliver   fell
They are verbs associated with midwives and lumberjacks.

4.   orbit   float
They describe how a planet and a cloud move.

5. PV
The first letter in the pair moves forward 3 letters, the second letter moves forward 4 letters.

6. GO
The first letter in the pair moves back 1 letter, the second letter moves back 5 letters.

7. PM
The first letter in the pair moves forward 3 letters, the second letter moves back 6 letters.

8. OT
FA and UZ are mirror pairs, where the two letters are an equal distance from the centre of the alphabet. O is the mirror of L and T is the mirror of G.

9. primrose
'primrose' is the only correctly spelled word that can be made.

10. deadlock
'deadlock' is the only correctly spelled word that can be made.

11. tendon
'tendon' is the only correctly spelled word that can be made.

12. sideboard
'sideboard' is the only correctly spelled word that can be made.

13. 21
Add the two outside numbers together.

14. 12
Divide the first number by the second number and then add 6.

15. 4
Divide the first number by the second number and then subtract 2.

16. 30
Multiply the first number by 2 and then add the second number.

Test 17 — pages 42-43

1. HIM
The complete word is THIMBLE.

2. OLD
The complete word is FOLDERS.

3. POT
The complete word is SPOTLIT.

4. MAT
The complete word is AMATEUR.

5. unleash restrain
'unleash' means 'to let loose', whereas 'restrain' means 'to hold back'.

6. draconian merciful
'draconian' means 'harsh', whereas 'merciful' means 'forgiving'.

7. forlorn jovial
'forlorn' means 'sad', whereas 'jovial' means 'happy'.

8. acclaim infamy
'acclaim' means 'praise for a good quality', whereas 'infamy' means 'reputation for a bad quality'.

9. let
Take letter 3 from the second word, followed by letters 2 and 1 from the first word.

10. fad
Take letter 3 from the second word, followed by letters 2 and 4 from the first word.

11. dew
Take letters 4 and 3 from the first word, followed by letter 4 from the second word.

12. are
Take letters 2 and 3 from the second word, followed by letter 4 from the first word.

13. DZ
The first letter in the pair moves forward 3 letters each time. The second letter moves forward 2 letters each time.

14. UR
The first letter in the pair moves forward 2 letters. The second letter moves back 4 letters.

15. EC
The first letter in the pair moves forward 3 letters. The second letter moves in the sequence -1, -2, -3, -4, -5.

16. UZ
The first letter in the pair moves in the sequence +1, +2, +3, +4, +5. The second letter moves in the sequence -2, -1, -2, -1, -2.

Test 18 — pages 44-45

1. hamper hinder
Both of these mean 'to obstruct'.

2. provoke goad
Both of these mean 'to make someone angry'.

3. flourish thrive
Both of these mean 'to prosper'.

4. mundane monotonous
Both of these mean 'boring'.

5. 6524
D = 6, R = 5, A = 2, G = 4

6. 1641
E = 1, D = 6, G = 4, E = 1

7. AREA
A = 2, R = 5, E = 1, A = 2

8. t
The new words are 'cast', 'teem', 'goat' and 'tour'.

9. h
The new words are 'rich', 'hats', 'high' and 'hymn'.

10. m
The new words are 'seem', 'meek', 'palm' and 'made'.

11. p
The new words are 'flap', 'port', 'clap' and 'paid'.

12. d
The new words are 'curd', 'dear', 'card' and 'dial'.

13. RU
Both letters in the pair move forward 3 letters.

14. MT
The first letter in the pair moves forward 4 letters each time. The second letter moves back 2 letters each time.

15. RI
The first letter in the pair moves in the sequence −2, +1, −2, +1, −2. The second letter moves in the sequence +1, +2, +3, +4, +5.

16. VP
The first letter in the pair moves in the sequence −2, −4, −6, −8, −10. The second letter moves in the sequence +3, +4, +3, +4, +3.

Puzzles 5 — page 46

Triangle Teasers

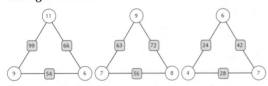

Sudoku School

N	E	A	T	D	I	U	C	O
D	O	T	N	U	C	A	E	I
C	I	U	O	A	E	D	T	N
E	A	D	C	O	N	I	U	T
T	U	I	D	E	A	N	O	C
O	N	C	U	I	T	E	A	D
I	D	O	A	T	U	C	N	E
A	C	E	I	N	O	T	D	U
U	T	N	E	C	D	O	I	A

Test 19 — pages 47-49

1. tile
Rearrange letters 2, 3, 4 and 5 in the order 5, 2, 3, 4.

2. cone
Rearrange letters 1, 2, 4 and 5 in the order 1, 2, 5, 4.

3. each
Rearrange letters 1, 2, 3 and 5 in the order 5, 2, 3, 4.

4. girl
Rearrange letters 1, 3, 4 and 6 in the order 6, 4, 1, 3.

5. 8
$36 − 9 = 27, 27 = 19 + 8$

6. 2
$12 × 12 = 144, 144 = 288 ÷ 2$

7. 6
$16 + 7 − 5 = 18, 18 = 3 × 6$

8. 3
$47 + 3 ÷ 2 = 25, 25 = 75 ÷ 3$

9. virus   flu
The other three are what you might do if you have a virus or flu.

10. swimming   diving
The other three are water sports that require a boat.

11. imperil   jeopardise
The other three mean 'to end the existence of'.

12. reckless   blasphemous
The other three mean 'severe'.

13. B
Sabiha came second, which means Alicia must have finished first. Will finished last (fifth). Dan didn't finish fourth, so this means he must have finished third, meaning that Rodolfo finished fourth.

14. D
There is 1 dark egg and 1 white egg at the tree. There is 1 dark egg and 1 milk egg in the shed. There is 1 dark egg in the rose bush. There are 2 milk eggs in the vegetable patch. There is 1 dark egg and 2 white eggs at the pond. Therefore, it must be true that there are 6 milk and white eggs in total.

Test 20 — pages 50-51

1. LAP
The complete word is CLAPPING.

2. HIT
The complete word is WHITENED.

3. PIP
The complete word is BAGPIPES.

4. OIL
The complete word is RECOILED.

5. pluck   fillet
The other three are ways of cooking something.

6. prepay   forethought
The other three are things that happen after an event.

7. advance   upgrade
The other three mean 'to move to a lower rank or position'.

8. readers   listeners
The other three watch something.

9. leap
The word is hidden in the phrase 'icicle appeared'.

10. item
The word is hidden in the phrase 'mite managed'.

11. sale
The word is hidden in the phrase 'salsa left'.

12. hear
The word is hidden in the phrase 'the army'.

13. tree
The word is hidden in the phrase 'great reef'.

14. 5412
R = 5, A = 4, I = 1, N = 2

15. 5136
R = 5, I = 1, F = 3, E = 6

16. FINE
F = 3, I = 1, N = 2, E = 6

Test 21 — pages 52-53

1. KIT
The complete word is SKITTLES.

2. COW
The complete word is SCOWLING.

3. CAN
The complete word is VACANTLY.

4. PIT
The complete word is SPITEFUL.

5. 89
Add 7 each time.

6. 25
Divide by 2 each time.

7. 17
There are two sequences which alternate.
In the first sequence, add 4 each time.
In the second sequence, add 3 each time.

8. 6
There are two sequences which alternate.
In the first sequence, add 1 each time. In the
second sequence, subtract 2 each time.

9. real fake
'real' means 'genuine', whereas 'fake' means 'not genuine'.

10. cryptic clear
'cryptic' means 'confusing', whereas
'clear' means 'easily understood'.

11. spontaneous planned
'spontaneous' means 'occurring on impulse',
whereas 'planned' means 'arranged in advance'.

12. disgusting delectable
'disgusting' means 'horrid', whereas
'delectable' means 'delicious'.

13. COME
To get from the code to the word, move the
letters in the sequence −3, −4, −3, −4.

14. SAVE
To get from the code to the word, move the
letters in the sequence +1, +0, −1, −2.

15. JMSB
To get from the word to the code, move the
letters in the sequence +4, −5, +4, −5.

16. EPAM
To get from the word to the code, move the
letters in the sequence +2, +4, +6, +8.

Test 22 — pages 54-55

1. EWE
The complete word is FAREWELL.

2. CAR
The complete word is SCARED.

3. FIN
The complete word is INFINITE.

4. RUE
The complete word is GRUESOME.

5. E
$6 \times 4 = 24$, E = 24

6. C
$72 \div 6 + 4 = 16$, C = 16

7. E
$7 \times 3 + 6 = 27$, E = 27

8. B
$4 \times 2 + 9 - 13 = 4$, B = 4

9. students congregation
They are the people who are lectured and preached to.

10. market auction
They are places where people barter and bid for items.

11. ancestor descendent
They describe what a grandparent and a child are.

12. unobtrusive shy
They are synonyms for 'discreet' and 'demure'.

13. 9
$39 - 16 = 23$, $23 = 14 + 9$

14. 3
$9 \times 8 - 22 = 50$, $50 = 150 \div 3$

15. 6
$4 + 15 - 7 = 12$, $12 = 2 \times 6$

16. 4
$64 \div 8 + 8 = 16$, $16 = 4 \times 4$

Puzzles 6 — page 56

Compound Conundrums

MILKSHAKE, BACKFIRE, BUTTERFLY,
CATWALK, WATERFALL, WIDESPREAD,
HAIRCUT, DAYBREAK, HOUSEHOLD

Test 23 — pages 57-59

1. s
The new words are 'class', 'sale', 'loss' and 'said'.

2. y
The new words are 'bony', 'year', 'ally' and 'your'.

3. f
The new words are 'leaf', 'fate', 'chef' and 'fist'.

4. n
The new words are 'main', 'nose', 'down' and 'nets'.

5. polish
'polish' can mean 'to make shiny' or 'to add
the finishing touches to something'.

6. cap
'cap' can mean 'to curb' or 'to put a lid on something'.

7. press

'press' can mean 'to apply pressure to something' or 'to persuade someone to do something.'

8. motion

'motion' can mean 'a movement to express a meaning' or 'a proposition'.

9. i

The new words are 'weld' and 'said'.

10. g

The new words are 'ripe' and 'gore'.

11. c

The new words are 'with' and 'cape'.

12. e

The new words are 'clan' and 'hide'.

13. E

The sprouts are at the centre of the circle. Going from the sprouts to the outer edge of the circle, the vegetables are ordered as follows: sprouts, parsnips, cabbages, carrots and potatoes. Therefore, it cannot be true that two rings of vegetables separate the potatoes from the sprouts.

14. C

'Cookery Capers' starts at 9 am and lasts 90 minutes. Therefore, it finishes at 10.30 am. 'Ruthless Referees' is on from 10 am to 11 am. 'Emotional Street' starts 1 hour after 'Cookery Capers' starts, ending at the same time as 'Ruthless Referees'. Therefore, 'Emotional Street' is also on from 10 am to 11 am. Jarvis can record just 1 programme at a time. Therefore, if he watches all of 'Cookery Capers', he could record either 'Emotional Street' or 'Ruthless Referees', but he would miss 30 minutes of the programme he doesn't record.

Test 24 — pages 60-61

1. r

The new words are 'acid' and 'drew'.

2. d

The new words are 'bran' and 'axed'.

3. e

The new words are 'very' and 'tube'.

4. s

The new words are 'beat' and 'pies'.

5. beef   bacon

They are terms for meat that have been sourced from a cow or a pig.

6. flavour   ladle

They are synonyms for 'season' and 'spoon'.

7. harvest   abstain

They are antonyms for 'sow' and 'indulge'.

8. stoke   draw

They are verbs associated with a fire or a curtain.

9. 15

The numbers follow the sequence -6, -5, -4, -3, -2.

10. 45

Add prime numbers: + 2, +3, +5, +7, +11, +13.

11. 18

There are two sequences which alternate. In the first sequence, add 2 each time. In the second sequence, subtract 4 each time.

12. 32

There are two sequences which alternate. In the first sequence, multiply by 2 each time. In the second sequence, divide by 2 each time.

13. WW

The first letter in the pair moves forward 3 letters, the second letter moves forward 1 letter.

14. NJ

KP and IR are mirror pairs, where the two letters are an equal distance from the centre of the alphabet. The answer will be the mirror pairs for M and Q, which are N and J.

15. GE

The first letter in the pair moves forward 6 letters, the second letter moves forward 3 letters.

16. KH

The first letter in the pair moves back 7 letters, the second letter moves back 5 letters.

Test 25 — pages 62-63

1. gown

Rearrange letters 2, 3, 5 and 6 in the order 6, 2, 3, 5.

2. deer

Rearrange letters 2, 3, 5 and 6 in the order 3, 2, 5, 6.

3. more

Rearrange letters 2, 3, 5 and 8 in the order 3, 2, 5, 8.

4. pear

Rearrange letters 1, 2, 5 and 6 in the order 2, 6, 1, 5.

5. line

Rearrange letters 2, 3, 5 and 6 in the order 3, 2, 5, 6.

6. triumph   victory

Both words mean 'success'.

7. unanimous   united

Both words mean 'in complete agreement'.

8. correspond   communicate

Both words mean 'to liaise'.

9. unscrupulous   immoral

Both words mean 'unethical'.

10. B

$26 - 18 = 8, B = 8$

11. B

$18 \div 3 - 3 = 3, B = 3$

12. A

$7 + 9 - 10 = 6, A = 6$

13. D

$8 \div 2 \times 3 - 6 = 6, D = 6$

14. 3426

$N = 3, E = 4, A = 2, R = 6$

15. 1256

$L = 1, A = 2, I = 5, R = 6$

16. AREA
A = 2, R = 6, E = 4, A = 2

Test 26 — pages 64-65

1. rock
'rock' can mean 'a piece of hard material found on the ground' or 'to move from side to side'.

2. shuffle
'shuffle' can mean 'to reorganize' or 'to walk slowly'.

3. found
'found' can mean 'to set up' or 'came across'.

4. gorge
'gorge' can mean 'a narrow valley between hills or mountains' or 'to greedily eat a large amount of food'.

5. QK
The first letter in the pair moves back 3 letters, the second letter moves back 5 letters.

6. JV
The first letter in the pair moves back 2 letters, the second letter moves forward 2 letters.

7. NH
The first letter in the pair moves forward 8 letters, the second letter moves forward 5 letters.

8. SO
The first letter in the pair moves back 4 letters, the second letter moves forward 6 letters.

9. heartburn
'heartburn' is the only correctly spelled word that can be made.

10. broadband
'broadband' is the only correctly spelled word that can be made.

11. counterpart
'counterpart' is the only correctly spelled word that can be made.

12. restrain
'restrain' is the only correctly spelled word that can be made.

13. II
The first letter moves back 2 letters each time. The second letter moves back 3 letters each time.

14. DS
The first letter moves in the sequence −4, −1, −4, −1, −4. The second letter moves in the sequence +4, −3, +4, −3 +4.

15. KZ
The first letter moves in the sequence +2, +1, +2, +1 +2. The second letter moves back 5 letters each time.

16. DX
The first letter moves in the sequence −3, −1, −3, −1 −3. The second letter moves in the sequence +2, +3, +2, +3, +2.

Puzzles 7 — page 66

A Shock for Mr Poole

The pupil who made Mr Poole jump was **Tarquin**. The spider made Mr Poole jump. Haji didn't have a spider, so it wasn't him. Miranda put on a monster mask, so it wasn't her. Rufus didn't have the spider either, so it wasn't him. Therefore, it must have been Tarquin who made Mr Poole jump.

What Letter am I?

a. g
Taking 'g' out of 'bridge' leaves the word 'bride'.

b. r
Taking 'r' out of 'marker' leaves the word 'maker'.

c. v
Taking 'v' out of the word 'duvet' leaves the word 'duet'.

Test 27 — pages 67-69

1. hero
The word is hidden in the phrase 'the rock'.

2. head
The word is hidden in the phrase 'the admiral'.

3. stun
The word is hidden in the phrase 'ghost under'.

4. chin
The word is hidden in the phrase 'catch in'.

5. vehicle   trolley
The other three are verbs that describe how an object can be set in motion.

6. base   comfort
The other three are verbs that mean 'to show approval'.

7. seat   hall
The other three are people in charge.

8. enquire   query
The other three mean 'demand'.

9. d
The new words are 'bead', 'dear', 'curd' and 'dark'.

10. c
The new words are 'talc', 'cite', 'disc' and 'core'.

11. d
The new words are 'bread', 'deal', 'dread' and 'deem'.

12. g
The new words are 'bring', 'gill', 'sing' and 'grate'.

13. C
In the passage, it says "Barley sews twice as many stitches as Carrie". Therefore, it must be true that Barley is not the slowest stitcher.

13

14. C

There are 5 roles in the play. Briana is a star. Joe is a tree. Neither Mary nor Lewis play a snowflake, so this must be Olga's role. Mary isn't the donkey, so this must be Lewis's role. Therefore, it cannot be true that the angel, which appears on stage at 18.19, is Lewis's role.

Test 28 — pages 70-71

1.   draw   write

They describe how sketches and drafts are made.

2.   dirt   crease

They are what washing and ironing are intended to get rid of.

3.   chatter   shiver

They describe how teeth and the body move when you're cold.

4.   itch   thirst

They make you want to scratch and drink.

5.   ERDW

To get from the word to the code, move each letter forward 3.

6.   GOAT

To get from the code to the word, move the letters in the sequence -1, -2, -3, -4.

7.   SZRO

This is a mirror code, where the letters are an equal distance from the centre of the alphabet. S is a mirror of H, Z is a mirror of A, R is a mirror of I and O is a mirror of L.

8.   SAND

To get from the code to the word, move the letters in the sequence -2, -4, -6, -8.

9.   nail

Take letters 4 and 3 from the first word, followed by letters 3 and 4 from the second word.

10.   same

Take letters 3 and 2 from the first word, followed by letters 1 and 4 from the second word.

11.   pill

Take letters 4, 2 and 1 from the first word, followed by letter 4 from the second word.

12.   song

Take letter 1 from the first word, followed by letters 1 and 2 from the second word, followed by letter 3 from the first word.

13.   AG

The first letter in the pair moves back 1 letter each time. The second letter moves forward 1 letter each time.

14.   KN

The first letter in the pair moves back 3 letters each time. The second letter moves back 2 letters each time.

15.   KN

The first letter in the pair moves in the sequence +3, +4, +5, +6, +7. The second letter moves back 5 letters then forwards 2 letters alternately.

16.   RB

The first letter in the pair moves in the sequence +2, +4, +2, +4, +2. The second letter moves back in the sequence -1, -2, -3, -4, -5.

Test 29 — pages 72-73

1.   d

The new words are 'plod', 'doll', 'mould' and 'doubt'.

2.   t

The new words are 'belt', 'tight', 'cult' and 'tall'.

3.   e

The new words are 'sole', 'east', 'mine' and 'ease'.

4.   b

The new words are 'slab', 'bale', 'lamb' and 'barn'.

5.   2314

T = 2, I = 3, M = 1, E = 4

6.   5364

L = 5, I = 3, V = 6, E = 4

7.   MITE

M = 1, I = 3, T = 2, E = 4

8.   precise   inexact

'precise' means 'accurate', whereas 'inexact' means 'not quite accurate'.

9.   pacify   perturb

'pacify' means 'to make calm', whereas 'perturb' means 'to unsettle'.

10.   prosper   languish

'prosper' means 'to thrive', whereas 'languish' means 'to grow weak'.

11.   disconnect   join

'disconnect' means 'to detach', whereas 'join' means 'to attach'.

12.   B

$7 + 10 - 12 = 5, B = 5$

13.   D

$1 \times 2 \times 3 = 6, D = 6$

14.   A

$1 \times 4 - 3 = 1, A = 1$

15.   C

$16 \div 4 \times 5 - 4 = 16, C = 16$

16.   C

$12 \div 3 \times 7 - 20 = 8, C = 8$

Test 30 — pages 74-75

1.   HER

The complete word is SHERBERT.

2.   OUR

The complete word is JOURNALS.

3.   CAP

The complete word is ESCAPED.

4.   ICE

The complete word is SLICED.

14

5.   24
The letters move forward in the
sequence +1, +2, +3, +4, +5.

6.   29
Add the two previous numbers together,
i.e. 3 + 4 = 7, 4 + 7 = 11 etc.

7.   6
There are two sequences which alternate.
In the first sequence, divide by 2 each time.
In the second, multiply by 2 each time.

8.   40
There are two sequences which alternate.
In the first sequence, multiply by 2 each time.
In the second, subtract 9 each time.

9.   show   performance
Both words mean 'a production on stage'.

10.   apprehend   seize
Both words mean 'to capture'.

11.   accost   confront
Both words mean 'to approach boldly'.

12.   sly   cunning
Both words mean 'deceptive'.

13.   ELUG
To get from the word to the code,
move each letter forward 3.

14.   BOLT
To get from the code to the word, move the
letters in the sequence -1, -2, -3, -4.

15.   VGOC
To get from the word to the code, move the
letters in the sequence +2, -2, +2, -2.

16.   SHIP
This is a mirror code, where the letters are an equal
distance from the centre of the alphabet. H is a mirror of
S, S is a mirror of H, R is a mirror of I and K is a mirror of P.

Puzzles 8 — page 76

Ski Lift

1.   SLANG   SLANT
The ladder is: SLING SLANG SLANT PLANT.

2.   STALL   SMALL
The ladder is: STALE STALL SMALL SMELL.

3.   HAIRS   PAIRS
The ladder is: HAIRY HAIRS PAIRS PAINS.

4.   GRAZE   CRAZE
The ladder is: GRADE GRAZE CRAZE CRAZY.
Hidden word: **scales**

Ski Race

Slalom: 11.13
The start times add 2 minutes each time.

Freestyle: 13.42
The start times follow the sequence
+1, +2, +3, +4, +5, +6.

Downhill: 16.21
The start times follow the sequence
+1, +3, +5, +7, +9, +11.

Ski jump: 18.00
Each start time increases by the difference between
the two previous start times added together.
17.39 -17.34 = 5, 17.47 - 17.39 = 8, so Jones's
start time will be 17.47 + 5 + 8 = 18.00.

Test 31 — pages 77-79

1.   sandbag
'sandbag' is the only correctly spelled
word that can be made.

2.   forget
'forget' is the only correctly spelled
word that can be made.

3.   sculptor
'sculptor' is the only correctly spelled
word that can be made.

4.   cargo
'cargo' is the only correctly spelled
word that can be made.

5.   ship
'ship' can mean 'to send' or 'a vessel
that travels on water'.

6.   cabinet
'cabinet' can mean 'body of advisers' or 'storage unit'.

7.   ground
'ground' can mean 'made into small particles'
or 'the surface of the earth'.

8.   frustrate
'frustrate' can mean 'to annoy' or 'to
prevent from succeeding'.

9.   A
Anouk has the second highest number of pens.
Gabe has more pens than Anouk. Therefore, Gabe
must have the highest number of pens. Elspeth
has more pens than both Iago and Alexei. Therefore,
Elspeth has the third highest number of pens.
Alexei has the fewest pens. Therefore, Iago must
have the fourth highest number of pens.

10.   B
The seats are arranged in four rows and the bus has
8 seats, so each row must contain two seats. On the
right-hand side, all the seats are taken. From front to
back, sit the driver, Konnie, Dan and Avril. Brian is sat
at the back on the left-hand side. Eli is sat in front of
Brian. So, Eli is sat in the third row from the front.

11.   17
Add the two outside numbers together and then add 1.

12.   9
The answer is the midpoint between
the two outer numbers.

13.   4
Add the two outside numbers together and then divide
by the first number.

14. 6
Add the two outside numbers
together and then subtract 2.

Test 32 — pages 80-81

1. mess
The word is hidden in the phrase 'James said'.

2. pope
The word is hidden in the phrase 'help open'.

3. rear
The word is hidden in the phrase 'Where are'.

4. tall
The word is hidden in the phrase 'about all'.

5. term
The word is hidden in the phrase 'after me'.

6. 35
The number added increases by 1
each time: +4, +5, +6, +7, +8.

7. 34
The two previous numbers are added
together to get the next number in the
sequence, i.e. 2 + 3 = 5, 3 + 5 = 8 etc.

8. 40
The numbers follow the sequence -2, 0, +2, +4, +6, +8.

9. 24
There are two sequences which alternate.
In the first sequence, add 4 each time.
In the second sequence, multiply by 2 each time.

10. theatre cinema
They are places where a stage and a screen can be found.

11. saw paintbrush
They are the tools a carpenter and a painter work with.

12. define calculate
They describe what a dictionary and a calculator do.

13. solve find
They are verbs which are associated
with a solution and a discovery.

14. 3421
S = 3, H = 4, O = 2, P = 1

15. 3125
S = 3, P = 1, O = 2, T = 5

16. SHOE
S = 3, H = 4, O = 2, E = 6

Test 33 — pages 82-83

1. b
The new words are 'land' and 'bare'.

2. l
The new words are 'pace' and 'glum'.

3. f
The new words are 'rile' and 'feel'.

4. n
The new words are 'mice' and 'hunt'.

5. 4
Divide the first number by the third
number and then add 1.

6. 16
Multiply the outside numbers and then divide by 2.

7. 14
Multiply the third number by 2 and then
subtract from the first number.

8. 10
Subtract the third number from the
first number and then divide by 3.

9. raisin prune
The other three are names of fresh fruits.

10. slide roll
The other three all mean 'to propel through the air'.

11. propose suggest
The other three all mean 'to accept'.

12. mature senior
The meaning of the other three is restricted to age.

13. RSHQ
To get from the word to the code,
move each letter forward 3.

14. BEAR
To get from the code to the word, move the
letters in the sequence -1, -2, -3, -4.

15. WHRC
To get from the word to the code, move the
letters in the sequence -5, -4, -3, -2.

16. CORD
This is a mirror code, where the letters are an equal
distance from the centre of the alphabet. X is a mirror of
C, L is a mirror of O, I is a mirror of R and W is a mirror of D.

Test 34 — pages 84-85

1. beat
Take letter 1 from the second word, followed
by letters 3, 4 and 2 from the first word.

2. felt
Take letter 4 from the second word, followed
by letters 3, 4 and 5 from the first word.

3. epic
Take letters 3 and 2 from the first word, followed
by letters 1 and 3 from the second word.

4. loft
Take letters 3 and 2 from the first word,
followed by letter 2 from the second word,
followed by letter 1 from the first word.

5. D
8 − 4 + 3 = 7, D = 7

6. E
11 × 2 + 12 = 34, E = 34

7.   C
$10 \div 5 + 2 - 1 = 3, C = 3$

8.   B
$60 \div 3 + 10 - 20 = 10, B = 10$

9.   6
The numbers follow the sequence -5, -4, -3, -2, -1.

10.   57
Add square numbers each time +2, +4, +9, +16, +25.

11.   7
There are two sequences which alternate.
In the first sequence, add 2 each time. In the
second sequence, subtract 4 each time.

12.   16
There are two sequences which alternate.
In the first sequence, multiply by 2 each time.
In the second sequence, add 3 each time.

13.   TY
The first letter moves forward 4 letters.
The second letter moves forward 5 letters.

14.   JU
The first letter moves forward 3 letters.
The second letter moves back 6 letters.

15.   OP
The first letter moves back 1 letter.
The second letter moves forward 5 letters.

16.   EH
This is a mirror code, where the letters are an
equal distance from the centre of the alphabet.
V is a mirror of E, S is a mirror of H.

Puzzles 9 — page 86

Word Grid

Mysterious Messages

a)   WHERE IS THE CHEESE?
To get from the code to the word,
move each letter back 3.

b)   I HAVE LOST MY MOUSE.
To get from the code to the word,
move each letter forward 4.

c)   THE CAT NEEDS A BATH.
This is a mirror code, where the letters are an equal
distance from the centre of the alphabet.

Test 35 — pages 87-89

1.   poet
Rearrange letters 1, 2, 4 and 5 in
the order 4, 2, 5 and 1.

2.   race
Rearrange letters 2, 3, 5 and 6 in
the order 6, 2, 3 and 5.

3.   reef
The last letter of the word moves forward
two places along the alphabet.

4.   earl
Rearrange letters 1, 2, 3 and 4 in
the order 4, 1, 2 and 3.

5.   5
$14 - 6 = 8, 8 = 3 + 5$

6.   2
$15 \times 2 - 8 = 22, 22 = 44 \div 2$

7.   8
$21 \div 7 + 9 = 12, 12 = 4 \times 5 - 8$

8.   2
$56 \div 8 - 1 = 6, 6 = 48 \div 12 + 2$

9.   recall   forget
'recall' means 'to remember', whereas
'forget' means 'to fail to remember'.

10.   modern   outmoded
'modern' means 'present-day', whereas
'outmoded' means 'old-fashioned'.

11.   doleful   exuberant
'doleful' means 'mournful', whereas
'exuberant' means 'cheerful'.

12.   aggravate   alleviate
'aggravate' means 'to make worse', whereas
'alleviate' means 'to make less severe'.

13.   B
Lola has more stripes than Sophie, and Sophie has the
second highest number of stripes. Therefore, it must
be true that Lola has the highest number of stripes.

14. D
After the pupils had learnt some Spanish,
they were able to say 'hello' in five languages,
including English. Therefore, Spanish must have
been the forth language the pupils learnt.

Test 36 — pages 90-91

1.   colleague   co-worker
Both words mean 'someone you work with'.

2.   resemblance   similarity
Both words mean 'likeness'.

3.   ransack   scour
Both words mean 'to search thoroughly'.

4.   antagonistic   hostile
Both words mean 'unfriendly'.

5. C
$18 - 9 = 9, C = 9$

6. D
$6 \times 8 = 48, D = 48$

7. A
$4 \times 3 - 11 = 1, A = 1$

8. D
$8 \div 4 + 6 = 8, D = 8$

9. chap
The word is hidden in the phrase 'church appointed'.

10. hare
The word is hidden in the phrase 'sixth arena'.

11. lump
The word is hidden in the phrase 'Plum pudding'.

12. newt
The word is hidden in the phrase 'knew too'.

13. KZRS
To get from the word to the code,
move the letters back 1 letter.

14. MEAL
To get from the code to the word, move the
letters in the sequence $-1, -2, -1, -2$.

15. ISTO
To get from the word to the code, move the
letters in the sequence $+2, +4, +6, +8$.

16. ROAD
To get from the code to the word, move the
letters in the sequence $-3, +4, -3, +4$.

Test 37 — pages 92-93

1. glove   blouse
The other three are worn on the feet.

2. mistletoe   holly
The other three are Christmas tree decorations.

3. recover   suffer
The other three are verbs associated with
the activities of medical professionals.

4. institution   company
The other three describe parts of an
institution or a company.

5. 1465
$R = 1, E = 4, A = 6, D = 5$

6. 5613
$D = 5, A = 6, R = 1, T = 3$

7. DEAR
$D = 5, E = 4, A = 6, R = 1$

8. wet
Take letter 1 from the second word, followed
by letters 2 and 1 from the first word.

9. cap
Take letters 3 and 2 from the first word, followed by
letter 2 from the second word.

10. nip
Take letter 3 from the second word, followed
by letter 3 from the first word, followed
by letter 1 from the second word.

11. kilt
Take letters 1, 2 and 3 from the first word,
followed by letter 1 from the second word.

12. feat
Take letters 1 and 2 from the second word,
followed by letters 2 and 3 from the first word.

13. 4
$34 - 6 = 28, 28 = 24 + 4$

14. 2
$6 \times 6 - 11 = 25, 25 = 50 \div 2$

15. 7
$15 + 6 - 7 = 14, 14 = 2 \times 7$

16. 12
$54 \div 9 \times 8 = 48, 48 = 12 \times 5 - 12$

Puzzles 10 — page 94

Word generator

Answers include: card, clad, sand, lend, land, lead, darn,
dale, ends, read, nerd.

Number Path

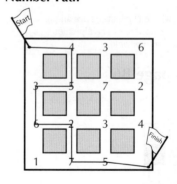

BLANK PAGE

BLANK PAGE